IMAGES OF WAR

The Germans on the Somme 1914-1918

RARE PHOTOGRAPHS FROM WARTIME ARCHIVES

DAVID BILTON

Pen & Sword
MILITARY

First published in Great Britain in 2009 by
PEN & SWORD MILITARY
An imprint of
Pen & Sword Books Ltd
47 Church Street
Barnsley
South Yorkshire
S70 2AS

Copyright © David Bilton, 2009

ISBN 978 1 84415 865 2

A CIP catalogue record for this book is
available from the British Library

Typeset by Phoenix Typesetting, Auldgirth, Dumfriesshire
Printed and bound in Great Britain by CPI UK

Pen & Sword Books Ltd incorporates the Imprints of
Pen & Sword Aviation, Pen & Sword Family History, Pen & Sword Maritime,
Pen & Sword Military, Wharncliffe Local History, Pen & Sword Select,
Pen & Sword Military Classics, Leo Cooper, Remember When, Seaforth Publishing
and Frontline Publishing

For a complete list of Pen & Sword titles please contact
PEN & SWORD BOOKS LIMITED
47 Church Street, Barnsley, South Yorkshire, S70 2AS, England
E-mail: enquiries@pen-and-sword.co.uk
Website: www.pen-and-sword.co.uk

Contents

Acknowledgements

"Not again, please!" and "Why are you writing another book?" were the common cries – sorry! Once again, a big and meaningful thank you to my family who have to put up with my need to write. Again, what would I do without Anne Coulson to read my proofs or the Prince Consort's Library to assist me in my research? Thank you. As always it was a pleasure to work with the wonderful team at Pen and Sword who are always so forgiving.

Errors of omission or commission are solely my responsibility.

Introduction

The Somme, Département 80, is part of Picardy, an area forever part of the greatest and worst of British military history in the Great War. But its historical importance was not manifest until July 1916 and then again in early 1918.

Although not in the original plans of the German Army, 'war came in earnest to the unspoilt, prosperous farming area of the Somme in the closing days of September' and stayed there for the duration of the war. After the initial battles between the French and Germans the region settled down to trench warfare in a modest way. It was not until the arrival of the British in July 1915 that the area became more active. A year later, with the first battle of the Somme, the area became, for nearly five months, strategically very important.

By the end of 1916 the German Army found its position in the region to be untenable and strategically withdrew, under the noses of the British, to new positions. Already, however, the focus of the war had changed with the French attacking further south and the British to the north, leaving the Somme a relatively quiet sector. It was not until March 1918 that full-scale war returned when the Kaiserschlacht began. On 1 July 1916, on the opening day of the great Somme offensive, the British army suffered its greatest death toll in one day, and, on 21 March, on the first day of the German offensive on the Somme, it suffered its greatest number of POWs taken. When the offensive 'ran out of steam', the British gradually retook the lost ground and by the last few weeks of the war the Somme again became a peaceful place.

German unit titles explain their origin and to some extent the ages of the men involved: Reserve units comprised men who had recently completed their compulsory service, Ersatz units were made up of physically fit men who had not been called up for conscript service, while Landwehr and Landsturm 'designated successively older age groups.' However, as the war progressed the names remained unchanged but the personnel did not always reflect the title. An Ersatz unit might contain anyone not in another unit at that particular time, and so spare to requirements and free to serve in a unit with a short life span. While German regiments were raised by the independent states and many had their own titles and number, apart from Bavarian troops, they were subsumed into the general structure. From 1915 onwards brigades were replaced by regiments of three battalions, making a German division roughly the same size as a British one.

France and Germany had been at war in the 1870s. A German postcard celebrating their victory at Bapaume in January 1871.

Chapter One

1914

After days of diplomatic discussion across Europe, following the death of Archduke Ferdinand, the first shots of the war were fired on 29 July when two Austrian monitors bombarded Belgrade and in return were shelled by Serbian guns on Topcider Heights. On the same day the German North Sea and Baltic fleets were mobilised and the British First Fleet sailed from Portland for Scapa Flow ready for their war station, as the British Cabinet pressed the German Government for mediation, warning that it could not stay out in all circumstances. At the same time Germany asked Britain to stay neutral, promising in return not to annex any French territory, while warning Russia that even a partial mobilisation would trigger war. Regardless of the warning, the next day the Russian Tsar signed the order for general mobilisation on 4 August.

On 31 July, Germany declared a 'state of danger of war' and demanded assurances of French neutrality within eighteen hours - these were not forthcoming. Before the day was out and war declared, Germany decided to mobilise; the cruiser Königsberg left Dar-es-Salaam to raid Allied commerce, Russian ships began mine-laying in the Gulf of Finland, Belgium ordered mobilisation for 1 August and Turkey ordered full mobilisation for men between twenty and forty-five for 3 August. At midnight the German Government declared an 'imminent danger of war' and issued ultimatums to France and Russia, asking the latter to end all military steps by noon 1 August, while the former was called upon to declare its intentions with regard to the Russo-German conflict.

Wanting to fight a war only on the Eastern Front, the Kaiser found, on 1 August, that mobilisation could not be confined to just one front. The same day France ordered a general mobilisation but, as preparations continued, the day was quiet until 1700 hours when Germany prematurely invaded Luxembourg, ordered general mobilisation for men aged twenty to forty-five and ten minutes later declared war on Russia. Although not at war, Germany detained British merchant ships at Hamburg, mobilised the High Seas Fleet and assembled two U-boat flotillas off Heligoland. After mobilising, Belgium declared that she would uphold her neutrality.

On Sunday, 2 August, Germany demanded passage through Belgian territory in

The main street through the village of Allaines during the winter of 1914. There may have been a war on but little had changed away from the front line.

To accommodate the large number of headquarters staff many châteaux were taken over and their occupiers, if they had not already previously left, were moved out. Some were better equipped than others; Château Aubencheul-au-bac, had a small tropical garden attached to the rear of the main house.

An estate worker at Manancourt Château who had fought in the war of 1870/71 against the occupying power.

order to anticipate a French attack while simultaneously invading Luxembourg and sending patrols into France. In response France sent troops to the Franco-Belgian border, believing that the German probes were a ruse, and also sent an army corps into Alsace to seize Mulhouse and Huningen and destroy Rhine bridges. With its mobilisation complete, Serbian raiders captured towns on the Austria-Bosnia border while Russian troops invaded East Prussia. In the Baltic, the German cruisers Magdeburg and Augsburg shelled Libau and laid mines, while in Britain the Admiralty ordered full mobilisation.

There was no turning back on 3 August when Germany declared war on France claiming that French planes had bombed Karlsruhe and Nurenburg; Belgium rejected the German ultimatum; the British government pledged armed support to Belgium in case of a German invasion declaring a general mobilisation, German cavalry crossed into Belgium and German troops invaded Russian Poland. At sea, although not yet at war, a German mine laid off Cuxhaven sank the British ship, SS San Wilfrido.

The next day, German cruisers shelled French Algeria before being chased off by British battlecruisers - this again, even though no state of war existed between the two countries; British ships left Scapa to stop the German fleet from breaking out, Germany declared war on Belgium and invaded on a fifteen-mile front with the Belgian army concentrating west of Liège to face the threat. In Britain army

Active service was hard on boots. Based at Manancourt, regimental cobblers repair damaged boots.

reserves and territorials were mobilised. The die was cast for a world war and when the British ultimatum to Germany expired at 2300 hours British time, Britain and Germany were at war – the first major European war for nearly a hundred years.

Increasing the scale of the conflict, on 5 August, Austria declared war on Russia;

Bapaume during the winter of 1914

„Der Kaiser spricht."

Eine schwereStunde ist heute über Deutschland hereingebrochen. Neider überall zwingen uns zu gerechter Verteidigung. Man drückt uns das Schwert in die Hand. Ich hoffe daß, wenn es nicht in letzter Stunde meinen Bemühungen gelingt, die Gegner zum Einsehen zu bringen und den Frieden zu erhalten, wir das Schwert mit Gottes Hilfe so führen werden, daß wir es mit Ehren wieder in die Scheide stecken können. Enorme Opfer an Gut und Blut würde ein Krieg vom deutschen Volk erfordern. Den Gegnern aber würden wir zeigen, was es heißt, Deutschland anzugreifen. Und nun empfehle ich Euch Gott! Jetzt geht in die Kirche, kniet nieder vor Gott und bittet ihn um Hilfe für unser braves Heer!"

The Kaiser's speech to the German people on the eve of war with France explaining that 'A heavy time is today over Germany.'

in a quid pro quo, Montenegro declared war on Austria and Zanzibar declared war on Germany. Fighting on the western front continued with German forces failing to break Belgian resistance at Liège but managing to get through to Namur. On the North Sea, British cruisers sank the German minelayer Königin Luise off the Suffolk coast with two of the mines laid sinking the British cruiser Amphion.

The battles of the French frontiers began on 6 August, the same day that Serbia declared war on Germany. A day later, and only three days after declaring war, an advance party of the BEF landed in France with two corps following on 9 August, and by 16 August the entire expeditionary force was in France.

'On 1 August, just before 1900 hours, the time set for *16 Division* to move into Luxembourg, the Kaiser countermanded the order, but by then a company of *69 Infantry Regiment*, commanded by Lt. Feldmann, had already crossed the border and taken their objective; the next day *Fourth Army* occupied the country. Next day, the Belgian government refused the German army entry and, from that point on, considered itself to be at war with Germany. On 4 August German forces crossed the frontier, meeting little opposition.'

'While the German armies fought their way through Belgium, the French

During the initial battles on the Somme, before the lines settled down into trenches, any surviving buildings were used as a barracks, even churches.

When timber was available, Pioneer units were able to construct mass bunks so troops had a permanent place to rest and leave their belongings when at rest.

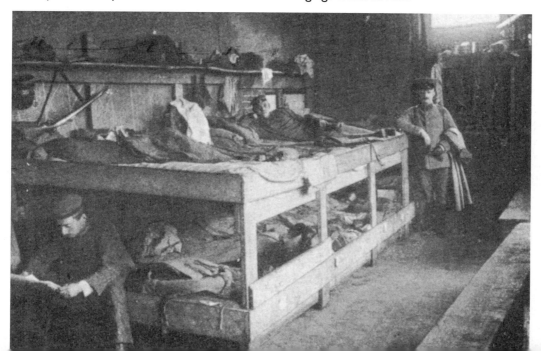

Officers were quartered in better billets and provided with a batman to look after their needs. In a larger billet like a château, they also had their own private orchestra.

A soldier from Ernst Junger's regiment – 73 Fusiliers, photographed just before setting off for the war. The regiment had served with the British Army during the siege of Gibraltar in the 18th century and wore a Gibraltar armband to commemmorate the action.

Wherever the ground was flat, it was necessary to provide as high an observation point as possible, in this case a platform built into a very tall tree.

French troops in bivouac on the Somme region.

launched their own attacks in Lorraine, the Ardennes and on the Sambre. No matter how valiantly the French and Belgians fought, the German army kept moving forward. On 24 August, 'one million Germans invaded France. For the French and British the great retreat had begun. It lasted for thirteen days, blazing summer days' in which the German Army made a bid for a swift decisive victory. 'They were desperate days for the Allies whose only offensive plan had not survived the opening battles of the war', while the German troops were following the highly detailed Schlieffen plan.'

'Five of the seven armies 'scythed down towards Paris on a 75-mile front. For the troops on both sides they were days of endless marching under a scorching sun.' Even though the Allied troops were under constant pressure their retreat was ordered and controlled, but each new action moved them closer to Paris – so close that, on 2 September, the French government left for Bordeaux.'

'However, a captured map shows that Kluck's First Army was now headed for the gap between the French Fifth and Sixth armies and not for Paris. This exposed his army's right flank to attack; this deviation from the Schlieffen Plan when his troops were seriously over-extended, badly exhausted and exposed, both on their flanks and the rear, resulted in a general withdrawal from the Marne to the Aisne.'

'With the Allied attacks failing to push the Germans back on the Aisne, attention on both sides was becoming increasingly concentrated on the open flank to the west, and, 'by the time the battle on the Aisne was dying down, activity at the western end of the line was developing fast.'

The end of the fighting on the Aisne brought about the final campaign of movement on the Western Front at the beginning of the war. Each side tried to outflank the other to the north, from the Aisne to the Somme through the Douai Plain and beyond. And as both sides raced towards the north, the various units involved leap-frogged past each other, taxing their lines of communication to the utmost in their efforts to move large bodies of troops to the north faster than the enemy could, but each manoeuvre ended in deadlock and trench lines.

Caught between the conflicts was Amiens, an important communications city for the French forces, with nine different railways joining in the city; strangely it was not a focal point in the attack on France, merely a town on the march to Paris. But during the move to outflank the French forces, Amiens became an accidental focus for both sides, as Arras did nearly a month later, with German victory followed by withdrawal.

After the battle of Charleroi, with von Kluck moving troops to outflank the retreating Allies, Amiens became a threatened town. At that time there was no specific defence of the biggest city in the Somme region apart from five French divisions situated between Dunkirk and Maubege with orders to check any cavalry

When the Germans attacked on the Somme those of military age left, leaving behind the young and old. Initially villagers kept their horses, but as losses increased it was necessary to requisition them to replace those lost to enemy action.

Somme-Py after the battle had moved on in 1914.

advance. Its front was so thinly held that when *I Army* arrived, they were obliged to fall back, leaving the area undefended. Amiens, whose strategic importance was realised by the French, was then occupied by Moroccan troops hurriedly despatched in the direction of Comon and Villers-Breton to organise defences. Their orders were to prevent a crossing of the Somme while the French 61 and 62 Divisions, who had previously pulled back to the northeast of Amiens, marched towards Péronne. However, their arrival at Bapaume was met with considerable resistance and after a day's fighting, the two divisions were thrown back northwards.

Further to the east, the French cavalry corps, supporting the British left wing, were unable to prevent the German advance from reaching the outskirts of Péronne on the evening of 27 August; the next day the town fell, with the cavalry corps moving south and the German Army marching on Amiens; by 29 August the German advance guards had reached Bray-sur-Somme, Chuignolles and Framerville. However the French moved a number of new battalions into the line and delivered a counterattack that not only inflicted numerous casualties but also took the village of Proyart. While this battle was under way, four territorial divisions moved up the Somme and established themselves in Amiens.

The next day, after a series of heavy counterattacks, the French troops pulled back leaving Amiens exposed and when the territorial divisions defending it evacuated the city, the way was open for its occupation. On 31 August the German Army entered the town requisitioning goods, food and money from the population to a value of 500,000 francs, and taking twelve town councillors and the Attorney-General hostage until 11 September when they were released.

'At first, the Imperial Army merely passed through Amiens on its forced march "nach Paris".' So between 1 and 9 September there were virtually no occupying troops in Amiens and those that did visit were officers ordered to requisition further materials and break open the safes of Savings Banks. However, on 9 September, a garrison was installed and a major appointed as town commandant. He imposed very restrictive orders on the French population that included injunctions, prohibitions and requisitions; 'it was forbidden to be in the streets after 8pm, or to sell newspapers. Motor vehicles were seized, and Frenchmen residing in Amiens who had not been mobilised, were ordered to the citadel. Two-thirds of them were eventually released, but about a thousand young men were sent away into captivity.'

Shortly afterwards, as a result of the Marne battles, the majority of the occupying troops left and when, on 12 September, French General d'Amande's advance guard entered the city, only a few prisoners were taken. For the next five days

Garrison and troops out on rest needed somewhere to go. Here a village hall has been taken over as a camp shop to provide the essentials of life, warmth, somewhere to talk and a small shop.

Cl. Duprès, Amiens

The church of the Golden Virgin in Albert after the German bombardment.

The first trenches were makeshift affairs with crudely dug sides, sacking covers and a little timber to hold up the earthworks.

French Territorial divisions secured the city and then moved onto the battles at Fricourt and Péronne that occurred later that month during the attempts by both sides to outflank each other. As each side held the other, the battle lines moved north and away in the direction of Arras and Flanders. Yet, while Falkenhayn continued to manoeuvre his troops on his right wing, he still focused on a possible push in the centre.

As the German troops pushed on the French positions on the Somme, the fighting was often fierce, confused, and backwards and forwards as the French moved reinforcements in to help take previously lost villages or parts of villages. The sudden appearance of field artillery on either side could quickly change the outcome. The fighting was to be among the last of its kind: 'cavalry patrols jingled and clattered round the countryside, reconnoitring and raiding' while 'infantry manoeuvred in close formation, shaking out only in the final stages of an attack.'

The result of such intense fighting was the usual one: a high level of casualties. These were too high for the medical services to deal with, and indeed, when the casualty rates for each year of the war are analysed, those for 1914 are the highest in the French and German armies. In the confused fighting, with little time to set up proper field ambulances or to clear the wounded, many were killed when a shell hit the temporary dressing station.

Two German cavalry corps were heavily involved in the September fighting: *1 Cavalry Corps* consisting of the *Guard* and *4 Cavalry Divisions* and *2 Cavalry Corps* made up of *2, 7* and *9 Cavalry Divisions*. Although involved in the fighting near Ham,

Christmas 1914 and a photo for the folks at home – whether the soldiers actually have a prisoner is not clear from the picture or the text which merely assures the reader that the writer is in good health, always.

Officers always got the best billets. A German postcard showing how officers lived in enemy territory.

Doullens was taken by the Germans in September 1914. This French postcard shows Uhlans walking through the town on their way to a more active area.

(Left) In the initial stages of the fighting in France anywhere was suitable for a billet as long as it offered some protection against the elements – here a church is providing a resting place for mounted troops.

Originalaufnahme vom Kriegsschauplatz.
Das Heldengrab am Straßenrain.

PHOTOCHEMIE,BERLIN
2873

(Left) Soldiers were buried where they fell in the aftermath of battle so single graves became a common sight in northern France until the war of movement was over and cemeteries were laid out.

Die Flucht der Engländer bei St. Quen

(Right) A rather far-fetched propaganda card showing the German cavalry routing British troops, dressed in colonial uniforms, near St. Quentin.

With the conflict moving backwards and forwards rapidly and then becoming trench bound, many of the dead were left unburied because to risk retrieving them would result in further death.

With the initial campaigns coinciding with harvest time, there were plenty of comfortable places to rest and observe the enemy. Here a haystack is being used as an observation platform with the troops waiting below for the order to advance.

Reservists proudly posing on their mobilisation just before the war began.

An unknown soldier poses by the rifles and packs of his comrades before being sent off to the front.

As stalemate developed, the destination of the infantryman became the trenches. Here soldiers march through a deserted village to the front.

AMIENS — Fugitifs.
Fugitives.

Not everyone stayed to look after their farms. As in the Second World War there were refugees, in this case moving away from the fighting in the Amiens area.

2 Cavalry Corps was moved to support *1 Bavarian Corps* that was pushing north. Moving off at 0530 hours on 25 September, *9 Cavalry Division* engaged the French at Chaulnes, taking numerous prisoners and threw the defenders back. Continuing on, it became involved with French infantry and artillery and was unable to make further progress because the attack by *1 Bavarian Corps* failed. However, *2 Cavalry Division* reached Herbécourt by 1400 hours and by the end of the day *7 Cavalry Division* had taken up positions at Cartigny, southeast of Péronne. The *Guard Cavalry,* after successfully engaging French cavalry near Péronne, was forced to withdraw in the face of strong French infantry attacks aided by artillery.

The next day *9 Cavalry Division* aided *1 Bavarian Corps* by clearing the woods south of Feuillères and the *Guard Cavalry Division* captured the area around Rocquigny after a cavalry charge. The *Guard Cavalry Division* was advancing on Mesnil when they came upon two French territorial companies retreating towards Rocquigny. *3 Guard Uhlan Regiment* sent three squadrons in succession against the enemy rearguard that consisted of both infantry and cavalry. Although their numbers were reduced due to casualties the squadrons couched their lances, wheeled into line and charged with loud "Hurrahs!" 'Half of the *5th squadron* plunged upon a retreating skirmish line, cutting down many of the Frenchmen in the hand-to-hand combat that ensued and sending others to the rear as prisoners.' The other half of the regiment turned left and overtook another retreating column and 'cut down a large number of the enemy, while shooting many of the remainder out of their saddles. *4 Squadron*, attacking on the right, 'fell upon the remnants of the hurriedly retreating rearguard…with such impact that many of the French were killed outright with the lance'.

Each day the cavalry were tasked with guarding the flanks of the attacking infantry. On 27 September they were assigned to *14 Reserve Corps* and *2 Bavarian Corps* where they fought at Longueval and Bazentin and further south they fought alongside *1 Bavarian Corps* at Flaucourt. Being mobile troops, the next day the corps fought at Courcelles, Achiet-le-Grand, Ervillers, Gomiécourt, Pys, Miraumont, Courcelette and Grandcourt. *7 Cavalry Division* seized Pys early that day and then assaulted French positions at Miraumont. At the end of the day, after heavy fighting under adverse artillery fire, assisted by *99 Reserve Infantry Regiment* and *2 Cavalry Corps* cyclist battalion, the town was in German hands and was retained against fierce counterattacks.

For a short while Amiens was held by the Germans but was evacuated before its significance was realised. Here German troops march through the city on 31 August.

French POWs being escorted from the battlefield.

Miraumont cemetery with soldiers' memorial at Christmas 1914.

Friedhof Miraumont.
nkmal für gefallene Kameraden
ingeweiht Weihnachten 1914

The fighting was not always in one direction with the French being pushed back. At Ervillers, resistance was too much for *4 Cavalry Division* who, even when supported by a brigade of the *Guard Cavalry Division,* were forced to retire. Although the *Guard Jaegers* and *3 Brigade* of the *Guard Cavalry* managed to hold the high ground between Bihucourt and Sapignies, the French recaptured Achiet le Grand and Gomiécourt only to lose them during the night when attacked by *Jaeger* and engineer patrols throwing grenades.

By 29 September, the situation of *I Cavalry Corps* had become critical when the French had outflanked its right wing. To assist, *9 Infantry Division* was ordered to break camp and move to Lagnicourt, where, together with *4 Cavalry Division* and the *Guard Cavalry Division* they were to mount a general offensive at 1400 hours against Croisilles, St. Léger, Ervillers and Gomiécourt. To further support the offensive, *14 Reserve Corps* was engaged in combat east of Albert and *2 Cavalry Corps* were to advance through Grevillers, Bihucourt and Miraumont.

The offensive met with mixed success. *7 Cavalry Division,* from *2 Cavalry Corps,* attacked Achiet le Grand but at 1000 hours was sent to assist on the right flank of *14 Reserve Corps* even though the attack had been met with success. When the division retired it left behind *15 Dragoon Regiment* and a company of cyclists to hold the positions they had taken. French artillery and infantry pushed the cavalry

Troops marching through the main square in Péronne during the autumn of 1914.

back out of the town. The *15 Dragoon Regiment* report emphasised how it was not possible to hold the position: 'the *4th squadron* reached the railway junction at Achiet le Grand. Their leader, Capt. Blume, desired to hold this village at all events, for the position commanded the road to Bapaume. Strong forces of the enemy cavalry were reported to the north on the heights of Gomiécourt and Courcelles, while their infantry, two battalions strong, were debouching towards us from Ablainzeville. Capt. Blume was reinforced by the *5th squadron* and a mixed detail from the cyclist company and the *4th* and *7th Jaegers*. The brave dragoons defended the northerly edge of the village under a heavy bombardment by the enemy. The led horses had to be brought farther to the rear for safety, yet deadlier grew the cannonading. Just then Capt. Blume arrived in the market place and prepared to climb the church steeple, where a junior officer, 2nd Lieut. Neufang, had been stationed for observation. The latter had succeeded in defining the position of the enemy batteries when a shot toppled the steeple, compelling him to descend from his post of observation. Another well-directed shot struck the tower, killing both officers…As their artillery ceased firing, the French began the

When the Germans arrived in Doullens in September 1914, they took the Mayor with them to requisition people's cars for use by the German Army.

Bapaume centre showing the damage caused by German shelling of the town.

assault. The *dragoons* and *Jaegers* slowly fell back before overwhelming numbers until they were finally driven from the place. Then it was discovered that the bodies of the officers had not been recovered. The field sub-surgeon, Dr. Steinborn, galloped in short order with the ambulance into the village, partly infested with the enemy, and courageously fetched the body of the captain, under continual fire from the French, but was compelled to leave 2nd Lieut. Neufang where he had fallen.'

The offensive at St. Léger had progressed favourably until an erroneous intelligence report from *7 Cavalry Division* indicated that *14 Reserve Corps* were falling back with heavy losses before overwhelming numbers of French infantry. *7 Cavalry Division* themselves were driven back towards Bapaume. This left the left wing of the *Cavalry Corps* exposed and when every outflanking movement failed the attack was called off and the divisions ordered to retire. As a result of the failed offensive and the lack of cohesion between the two corps, on 30 September they were merged under the control of General von der Marwitz except for *2 Cavalry Division* that stayed to guard the flank of *14 Reserve Corps* near Courcelette.

One of the many bridges that was blown by the French during the early stages of the Somme battles.

...sene Somme Brücke.

Christmas 1914 was celebrated in the trenches, as at home, with a Christmas tree.

Orders were once again issued for an offensive against French positions in Croisilles, St. Léger, Ervillers, Gomiécourt and Achiet le Grand. Three divisions from the newly amalgamated cavalry corps would advance simultaneously at noon. The offensive had an auspicious start and by the end of the day most of the objectives had been taken even though *2 Cavalry Corps* had halted their attack by 1800 hours.

'The offensive was to be carried on this day to act as a curtain to the movement of the *4th Army Corps* from Beugny northward to the region west of Vis en Artois on the main highway between Cambrai and Arras. This army corps had received orders to proceed against Arras in conjunction with the *1st Bavarian Reserve Corps*, which had arrived at Cantin, south of Douai.' No progress was made against strong French positions. Large bodies of troops were now moving north towards Arras. The battle was moving on from the Somme.

As the Bavarian troops pushed westwards in the direction of Albert, resistance stiffened even further and their over-hasty and sometimes uncoordinated attacks were no match for the well-positioned French infantry and their well-handled artillery. French resistance was stiffening across the region, and even the arrival of top quality divisions from other parts of the front, could not alter the balance enough to take villages like Fricourt without severe losses. The attacks continued but by 'the beginning of October the front line positions were starting to solidify as men dug and held where their advance had been checked.' However, 'these initial scrapes and trenches were rarely optimally placed and casualties continued to mount among the frontline forces.'

By 4 October the French position at Arras was threatened with encirclement. There were large gaps between units and Joffre was concerned that 2 French Army would withdraw south of the Somme exposing all the Allied forces in northern France. Realising that the operations in northern France now required more attention than he could provide, he appointed Foch as his deputy with control over the northern forces. Due to his vigorous approach, covering 850 kilometres within fifty-seven hours, he galvanised divisional, corps and army commanders so that by 6 October the Allied line from the Oise to north of Arras was secure. 'That evening Falkenhayn decided to cease all further attacks in Picardy; his attention – and that of Foch - was now moving north of Lens, to Flanders and the area between the River Lys and the sea.'

However, this decision did not stop the fighting on the Somme. Commanders became aware that there was no easy or simple way of moving west; the only solution was to continue local attacks and see what happened. One typical example was the attempt by *17 Infantry Regiment* to take Maucourt. Even though *17* and the supporting *131 Infantry Regiment,* were further reinforced by two companies on *97 Infantry Regiment* and a squadron from *7 Dragoon Regiment, by 1500 hours the attack* had failed. When darkness fell the survivors were ordered back to the start line leaving the stretcher-bearers to bring in the dead and wounded by moonlight.

The French XI Corps attacked Beaumont Hamel unsuccessfully on 19 November; it was a premonition of what was to come in 1916: the failure was blamed on insufficiently cut wire.

By the end of the year, the rapid victory imagined by the Central Powers and their enemies alike was a distant dream. On the Eastern Front the situation, although deadlocked, was felt to be temporary and more open to success by both sides, while on the Western Front siege warfare had become the norm with an almost unbroken, 400 mile long system of trenches on both sides of no man's land.

By the end of the year, after only five months of war, German casualties were nearly 120,000 dead and a further 400,000 wounded or POWs. The glorious adventure was over, but despite the military losses and the increasing hardship on the Home Front, the High Command claimed that victory would come in 1915 on the Eastern Front.

Chapter Two

1915

'As 1915 began the strategists of Germany and the Entente were thinking along similar lines. The results of previous offensives had convinced many leaders on both sides that if only a bit more pressure were applied, if only a bit more heavy artillery were employed, the enemy position would be broken through and mobility could thus be reintroduced to the war.' Once mobility had been restored it was assumed that the war could be won quickly and so both sides began preparing for an offensive to end trench warfare. However, the strength of the German positions made this unlikely for the Allies, and with German intentions focussed on the east the war was unlikely to be won in 1915 on the Western Front.

January started out cold, providing some respite from the mud, but when the rain arrived, the trenches quickly fell in, providing night and day repair work for men who were cold and hungry. Under the soil lay clay that became impervious to water drainage with the constant movement and, with no-where to drain, the water stayed in the trenches making movement and repair very difficult. Conditions were bad all month as one officer recalled: 'En route and in the communication trenches, the water was knee-deep in places. In the so-called shelters, the water dripped so much and so constantly that many simply avoided them, preferring to take their chances outside.' One officer, who was manning the telephone in a dugout when the snows suddenly melted, recalled 'a loud rushing noise as though a powerful stream was flowing past the door. I tried to see what it was but a clod of earth had jammed the door. At the same moment water began streaming in through cracks in the door, so fast that in three minutes I was standing up to my thighs in water. When I set about smashing the door in with a carbine, the water was suddenly up to my neck. I grabbed the telephone and climbed out and onto the parapet.' With no cover he and his men started to dig but found it difficult because their clothing was so stiff, and with the bad weather, it froze again, rusting the weapons.

The only comfort of the German soldier was that it was the same on the other side so each adopted a live-and-let-live approach that was only broken by the arrival of a new unit. A German officer later recalled the situation: 'Often we could

In many places cordial relationships existed between the villagers and troops. Here village children are having their jugs filled from the garrison field cooker.

As the trenches were established, many improvements were made to the lot of the troops with the introduction of normal household articles like tablecloths and tables. Stability also meant improved medical facilities. This photo shows the dugout of a medical officer, part of a foot artillery unit, somewhere under Serre.

A quiet day in May 1915. The Ancre before it became a major battleground.

A large house in Bapaume requisitioned for use by officers.

see that the ration parties were forced in the twilight to make their way across country outside the trenches, because over there, just as for us, to move through the trenches with food containers, weapons, loaves of army bread and similar items, was simply impossible. Who would hold it against us that in such situations we both acted as though we had seen nothing?' Towards the end of the month the weather became colder and when it froze, life again became bearable.

On 27 January, as was normal every year in the trenches, the Kaiser's birthday was celebrated, sometimes quietly like Christmas and at other times with offensive action but not necessarily an attack. On the sector of the Somme where the *Bavarian Leibregiment* were stationed a birthday celebration was arranged for the French. 'At exactly 12 o'clock the infantry along the entire line, as far as we could hear, opened up a rapid small arms fire on the enemy trenches. This was followed by a cannonade from the artillery, so it would have been possible to believe that a violent attack was about to take place. But, with the exception of a few nervous shot, the French let it pass without undertaking any sort of response.'

German engineering skills and ingenuity along with abundant defensive stores gave their troops a formidable defensive capability. This defensive stance for much of the war allowed them to concentrate on improving the sectors where terrain and time permitted. Larger shelters were built for the protection of the infantry in the line and much concrete was used to strengthen positions. The troops were well drilled in defensive tactics and resided in strengthened trench lines that were becoming semi-permanent homes, in some cases with stoves, tables and even pianos. Trench warfare was in their favour in 1915.

'The landscape dictated the methods used by the German Army. Labyrinthine redoubts...essentially underground strongholds, fortified villages and concreted machine gun and field artillery positions emerged on the chalk land regions of the Somme...where dugouts could be as much as forty feet deep.' Such constructions allowed many the comforts of electric lighting, piped water and air ventilation systems. However, such deep constructions could be safe havens from artillery shells but death traps when attacked by enemy infantry.

The conflict in 1915 would provide useful information to help make the defences even better. When the French had attacked near Hébuterne, the defenders secure in their deep dugouts did not have sufficient time to get out and engage the enemy who took them prisoner as they emerged. In order to stop this happening again General von Below issued an operational instruction directing that entrances

A column of ambulances waiting to move out to the battlefield to transport the wounded back to hospitals behind the front.

Beaulencourt decorated to celebrate the King of Württemberg's birthday.

Summer 1915. A gentle walk in the countryside past the Beaulencourt windmill on the road between Bapaume and Péronne.

Early summer 1915 in the trenches at La Boiselle, looking north from the village.

Nearly a year after the first battles and nearly a year to go before the next, the main road from Contalmaison to Bazentin.

were made wider, that each dugout should have two entrances and that they needed to be no deeper than three metres – sufficient to stop damage from any calibre up to 155 millimetre. Alarm systems were to be developed and tested so that men would know of an attack and every regiment was tasked with developing its own series of commands to make sure that dugouts emptied quickly and that everyone went immediately to their allotted station, with the soldier in charge of a dugout that failed to man its positions quickly enough facing court-martial for the offence.

Both sides patrolled each night to maintain contact with neighbouring units, check the wire and cover any gaps without generally bothering each other. However, such patrols slowly developed an aggressiveness that led them to become small raids against enemy standing patrols, listening posts and even the front line trenches, but every noise did not spell danger as *RIR 40* found out when a patrol of volunteers were sent out to check: nerves were strained expecting a

Late summer 1915. With a shortage of men to help with the harvest, German troops on rest help gather in the crops and thresh the corn.

Spring 1915. The view from the church tower in Flers, looking north down Wessigplatz.

French attack but the perpetrator proved out to be an umbrella blowing about.

Trench raiding provided the volunteers with aggressive action and sometimes a reward. On 17 January, the French trenches opposite *Landwehr Infantry Regiment 60* were more densely occupied than usual; the logical conclusion was that the French were about to attack, so volunteers were called for to find out what was happening. Unteroffiziers Koch and Wozniakowski, along with Musktier Selden climbed out of the trench with grenades and a trench knife in their boots; no rifles were taken. Passing the French sentry they reached the densely packed trench and immediately throw in their grenades: 'where they exploded, sending splinters flying in all directions. Loud shouts, confusion and frenzied shooting was the surprised response of the French troops.' Leaving the French to shoot at nothing, the three returned to their lines which immediately came under attack from the French artillery which killed some men in the Bunker where Koch was delivering his report. Incensed at the losses Koch took his party out again with a fresh load of grenades. Halfway across, the French, now very alert, fired, and wounded Koch who retired, leaving the others to continue their mission. After throwing their grenades into the still-packed trenches, they retired unhurt leaving behind a further memento of their escapade: 'The following morning a white flag was seen fluttering lustily from the French barbed wire obstacle, where Musketier Selden had tied it as a visiting card and token of German courage.'

As a result of the previous year's fighting there were many corpses lying unburied because of their closeness to the enemy's line; they were the missing of the Somme. Closeness and conditions dictated that they lay there rotting and stinking, until some way could be found to bring them for a decent burial. When the ground was covered in thick fog one February day, it gave one Feldwebel the chance to take a party out to remove some of the bodies. Rounding up any spare man with a spade they went out and buried nearly forty Germans who had died in the October fighting. Of these thirty were identified and their names and personal effects sent to divisional headquarters.

The village pond in Flers. Behind the pond, the undamaged church, in use as a field hospital, clearly shows a Red Cross symbol on its roof to prevent aerial attack.

Any large building could be used as a temporary field hospital. The church in Flers shown right, was used to accommodate sick, rather than wounded soldiers.

Mail, an essential part of a soldier's life, was sorted in base depots and then sent out to villages closer to the front before final transportation. Post, sorted in Bapaume, arrived at Flers for onward transport to the front line. To reduce the demands on manpower, the Germans used locals to transport the post. Here a young boy transports the mail using a donkey-pulled wagon.

The German war memorial in Flers.

The French were quick to take the offensive, but not on the Somme. Their chosen area was the Champagne region, where after a month and 240,000 casualties little progress had been made. The defenders had suffered only 45,000 casualties and, as a result, even though the number of available reserves was a pressing problem to *OHL,* the French had now lost the initiative. The problem for *OHL* was where to strike; three plans were carefully considered with each looking carefully for weaker, less well defended areas, suitable for a short, sharp artillery barrage and a rapid attack in large numbers, but events on the Eastern Front made the matter academic; there were not enough soldiers for an offensive on two fronts; if there had, the northern sector of the Somme could well have been involved as some sections of the French defences there fitted the German template for offensive of 'not more than average in strength, and in parts below average.'

Throughout 1915 there were numerous battles on the Western Front, gradually becoming larger and larger: Neuve Chapelle, Second Ypres (with the first use of poisonous gas in the west against the defending Allied troops), Aubers Ridge, Festubert and Loos in the British sector and Champagne, the Aisne, the Vosges, 2nd Artois, Champagne and 3rd Artois on the French sector but no major attacks on the Somme. Each of these attacks made the defenders ever more adept at dealing with the initial penetration of their defences through the rapid use of counter-attacks and artillery fire to disrupt the attacker's attempts to move on.

The defensive battles led to tactical innovation on a small unit scale. As a result of the work of Hauptmann Rohr, storm troops were being trained as assault detachments. These section-sized squads were taught to advance independently across no man's land and infiltrate rather than attack, using specialist weapons; they would play a part, just as the fortifications would, in the battle of 1916 on the Somme.

With the only strategic city, Amiens, some considerable distance behind French lines, the Somme Front was relatively quiet, and any attacks by both sides were of only local significance. It was not until June that the French increased their activity and shortly afterwards left the area for the British.

It might have become a minor front but the war did not stop. In some places the trenches were only 150 metres apart and were looked down upon by French infantry with sniping as a constant problem. The French troops in their deep trenches watched the constant barrage of their back positions and waited for the attacks that never came. When they were able to look at of their trenches, the view was not pretty. As a French sergeant described in a letter home in January, 'In front of our trench, about 100 metres away, there are the bodies of

The divisional canteen at Gomiecourt.

An idyllic view, Grandcourt near Miraumont with Hill 127 in the background. Seen from the ground (right) the picture tells a different story.

For the villagers that stayed on, life continued as it had always done – business as usual. Here German troops leave the Café du Nord in Grandcourt sometime in May 1915.

Four views of Grandcourt village during the summer of 1915, showing clockwise from right the Café du Nord in use as an officer's mess, the effect of large calibre shells on houses on the road to Thiepval, a requisitioned farm and the side of a house painted with a map to show the main theatres of operations.

Two views of Longueval, the main street in August 1915 and the grave of a French officer killed in 1914.

(Below) A gentle route march for the lightly wounded troops recovering at the Field Hospital in Manancourt.

The village pond in Le Mesnil was used by civilians and military to water their animals. The shortage of horses in the German Army is clearly here by the use of oxen.

A year after the battle had moved on most of the damage to roads and bridges had been repaired, even if only temporarily. To keep the army supplied a replacement wooden bridge was constructed on the northern exit from Martinpuich heading towards Courcelette.

Germans killed in a previous attack. There about fifty of them, all of them cut down by our machine guns.'

The year started with a successful French attack on positions near Vermelles followed by a further French attack resulting in a limited advance north of the river at La Boiselle. One hotly contested area at La Boiselle was Granathof (Glory Hole when the area was taken over by the British), an area of little tactical significance, more a matter of honour on both sides. Here sappers of both sides pushed out underground galleries in an attempt to blow the other side up; both sides could hear each other, work out where the other was but neither side knew when the other was going to detonate their explosives.

On 12 January the German miners exploded a 600 kilogram charge under the French positions, killing over forty men. According to an eyewitness the air was full of dismembered bodies and flying limbs, ten dead soldiers landing in front of the German front line while one soldier was blown to a height of 150 metres. Then, on 18 January, *RIR 120* attacked and annihilated two companies of French infantry and captured three officers and 104 men. The property was by now a

A well cared for, French mass grave, at the eastern end of the comparatively unscathed village of Le Transloy, for forty-four soldiers killed in the August 1914

wasteland but continued to be contested throughout the year.

On 3 February French troops witnessed an unusual sight when incendiary filled boats were floated across the Ancre in an attempt to dislodge them from their positions; all units held fast and in April there was heavy fighting near Albert.

There were also aircraft raids to get used to. Typically, passing aircraft attacked French positions looking for targets of opportunity. In his diary, one French soldier noted an attack around Bray on 4 June that resulted in machine guns and artillery firing for some considerable time with no effect. Bray was a regular target for bombing and the troops were not always as lucky as on 4 June. On 22 June the aircraft struck again, this time resulting in one soldier killed and many wounded. Bray was also a regular target for artillery fire and other incidents. On 23 June, after a spectacular fire, trench rumour suggested that it was as a result of espionage.

As everywhere else on the front, there were rats: 'the weather was very bad and the rats gave us a lot of trouble in the dugouts. Every time we came off sentry duty, or had returned from digging, dog-tired and just wanting to lie down straight away for a few hours' sleep, we were plagued by these beasts, half the size of rabbits, which came creeping up to sniff around for anything edible in our knap-sacks, which we used as pillows. They were not shy about using our faces as a shortcut, they scrabbled their way up the sleeves of our jackets and began to nibble away wherever they liked. These bloody creatures could drive a man to despair and for every dozen that we beat to death or shot, another dozen members of this noble race would take their place.'

Artillery bombardments were a constant threat on both sides, causing noise but

Three views of Montauban eighteen months before the 1916 offensive showing the destruction caused by French shelling and in contrast a way side cross.

By the summer of 1915, the disused railway station at Montauban was being reclaimed by nature.

not always the destruction that was intended. A French soldier noted a barrage in May that started at exactly 8pm and continued with only a forty-five minute break until midnight when it abruptly stopped. The targets were the French second and third line positions which were completely unaffected by the whole bombardment. However, a few days later, the bombardment was more accurate, hitting the frontline and blowing him off his chair in a dugout. There were also trench raids to deal with; the same soldier had written home the day before, and in reply to his wife's request about his three friends, merely told her that they were prisoners, and that the previous nights bombardment had wounded two and buried three of his other comrades.

Mining was commonplace on both sides of the wire but it did not always kill only the enemy. One French soldier who spent over eight hours helping complete preparations for a mine explosion recorded that they had created an impressive firework display that resulted in an artillery barrage on both sides. The next day they counted the cost of the retaliatory barrage: 7 Company – two dead and seven wounded, while 6 Company had six wounded.

Mines were lethal, as was the counter barrage, and digging the tunnels could also be dangerous. Only three days after the last mine, counter-mining troops managed to get into the French tunnel as they were finishing off and, after a terrible underground fight, over twenty men were dead or wounded. The final result was a terrible bombardment on both sides and, when a couple of days later they tried again, the result was the same: half a section of troops lost to the German bombardment.

On 12 April, on Hill 110, just south of Fricourt, an intense French artillery barrage started at 1000 hours; underneath, French engineers had set a large mine to explode one hour later. When it exploded it made a crater eight metres deep and twenty metres across, destroying a German gallery and a section of trench. This was followed by an unsuccessful attempt to take the crater. German losses were considerable: 'the mine had crushed the biggest dugout, burying twelve reservists, the Feldwebel and the platoon commander. After frantic digging they reached the men only to find them all dead.' The amount of mining is shown by the activity around La Boiselle in an eight-month period – sixty-one explosions with charges of up to 25,000 kilograms.

The comparative quiet of the last three months, compared with sectors like Arras and Ypres, was broken on 7 June, when parts of the French XI Corps attacked and captured the salient at Touvent Farm between Hébuterne and Serre on a front of two miles. The French attack aimed to reduce a salient to the west of Serre, but the ridge on which Serre stood was of great importance to the German positions so two infantry divisions were used to counter the attack and every reserve available was brought forward. The attack build-up had been clearly

A garden house in Miraumont hiding an underground bunker.

The view from the trenches at Ovillers looking towards La Boiselle.

observed from the air and so was expected, but the severity of the assault came as a surprise. After a three-day bombardment, exploiting the dense early morning fog in the same way as the Germans would in 1918, the French troops quickly took Touvent Farm and advanced on Serre, but were then repulsed. Four further assaults took place during the following week and although a strong German counterattack was beaten off, the attack was called off on 13 June when there was no realistic prospect of the high ground around Serre being taken.

Even with the French attacks in early 1915, the Somme had still been a relatively quiet sector with both sides adopting a live-and-let-live policy above ground wherever possible; little initially changed when the British arrived. On 13 July, the newly formed British Third Army relieved the French Second Army of a fifteen-mile sector from the River Somme to Hébuterne to the surprise of the German soldiers facing them, although observers had noted a continual increase in the amount of traffic and troop movement indicating a relief operation. Then the noise of the shells changed, as did the calibre and type of shell as well as the accuracy of the shelling; this now seemed designed to saturate an area rather than a specific target. Eventually empty shell cases showed who their new opponents were: the British. Shells made of drawn steel with thicker walls and thicker driving bands with rifling grooves different to French artillery, and obvious factory markings clearly showing they had been made in America or Britain. The British artillery had relieved the French and when a steel-jacketed bullet with five left handed rifling grooves appeared it was clear that British infantry had also arrived. But had they replaced the French, or was it a mixed force?

Even with the munitions and sightings of different uniforms there was still a need to confirm that they were British, so trench raids were needed, especially as the new residents were not yet out and about in no man's land. Then an enemy soldier who had become lost after working in no man's land appeared in front of the German trench. Upon being spotted, he was quickly taken prisoner and identified as British; further confirmation was provided later that day when a Scottish soldier was also captured.

This confirmation led to warnings of how underhanded Indian troops, that had been fighting alongside their British counterparts since the start of the war, could be – pretending to desert and then throw bombs, and to be wary of white flags being used by one unit and ignored by the next. In admitting that the British soldier was both daring and brave, regimental orders warned soldiers to be especially careful of wounded soldiers who would try and knife them as they were surrendering.

It might have been comparatively quiet, with the focus being to the north around Arras where many Somme-based soldiers were sent, but every effort was made to strengthen the German positions and to blow up the enemy with mines. A Leutnant from *Reserve Infantry Regiment 109* recalled: 'Over time, at the cost of strenuous labour, which robbed us of our nights, we produced a first-class trench

Morval, July 1915, and soldiers relax on a home made field carousel.

The main square in Péronne in April 1915 showing the destruction caused by Allied artillery during the 1914 fighting.

Parts of the Somme were very wet all year round and so did need to be protected because they were mostly impassable. This photo shows a river area near Péronne.

The River Somme was used for the transport of goods and materials from the rear areas and for human cargo. Here a local woman punts down the river with male passengers.

system…which in our sector…eventually reached twenty-seven kilometres.' Another Leutnant observed that: 'the dugouts were well made and practically shell proof, which was just as well as there was much artillery fire'; dugouts that would stand the defenders in good stead when the Allies attacked in the coming year. As well as strengthening the defences, units trained hard and *XIV Reserve Korps* issued a notice for display in all dugouts that exhorted troops to do their best, as they were superior to any enemy.

Troops returning from Arras brought with them new skills that they taught to those who had stayed. Of particular importance was the grenade, which was now a safe weapon to use, after a safety cap had been placed over the cord pull to stop accidental detonation. They were shown how to use massed grenades to simulate drumfire to produce a defensive area, and how to regain control of a lost trench by bombing from traverse to traverse. Bombing teams were formed and trained, and so important had the grenade become that it was incorporated into sports day programmes, to improve accuracy and distance of throwing, when units were on rest.

Field hospitals were generally a safe distance behind the front lines so that they would not be shelled by accident. Here, ambulances arrive at Pronville Field Hospital with wounded from the battle front.

The time from the arrival of the British until the end of the year was classed by the German troops as a period of quiet without large scale military operations, but as one Landwehr Leutnant recorded: 'it was of course not really peaceful. Nightly fights between patrols…later these grew into trench raids and involved substantial numbers of assaulting troops and large quantities of ammunition.' There was always artillery fire to contend with and its damage to repair, and, as the British had more shells available, it was the Germans who did the lion's share of the repairing. When shells landed on the villages used for headquarters and troop rest, then 'revenge fire' was delivered on comparable British targets; eventually an unwritten understanding came into place between both sides - tit for tat. German shelling of Albert station resulted in retaliation on Irles Halt; when the British fired on Pozières the reply landed on Authuille.

The Somme in 1916 would become famous for its mud and for its artillery fire. Both were in evidence at the end of 1915 when Rifleman Mühmelt wrote home to his parents just before Christmas: 'here we have terrible rain day after day. The mud in the trenches reaches above the knees…please send me some foot wrappings and a few pairs of proper socks…Here artillery and machine gun fire goes on nearly all day on both sides…One man…was killed by shrapnel yesterday…Our company was in the same position for 10 days and we were shelled continuously…No one is safe for one moment. Here at our quarters several enemy aircraft bombarded our battalion offices and the orderly room.'

A new development that provided the German Army with much intelligence was the Arend and Moritz stations. These allowed their operators to intercept radio transmissions and listen in to enemy telephone conversations. This well kept secret, using both methods, allowed the Germans access to every order issued and enabled them to collect the names of the officers they were facing. To this pool of knowledge the information contained in captured documents and prisoner statements was added.

The Somme Front would become active again, but not yet, as many of the troops were sent there from Flanders to rest, and little in the way of serious active operations was undertaken. Planning was under way at the start of December that would change this.

A Somme offensive was first mooted on 6 December at a conference of Allied commanders at Chantilly. General Joffre selected the Somme area because that was where the British and French front lines met; it would also be a considerable advantage to attack the enemy on a front where for long months the reciprocal

Not every village was a ruin before the 1916 offensive. Sauchy-Lestrie had been little affected by the 1914 battles or the 1915 shelling as can be seen from this photo of the main street showing villagers and occupiers enjoying the spring air.

activity of the troops opposed to each other had been less than elsewhere – so was born the Battle of the Somme. 'Its drawbacks were that no great strategic objectives, such as rail centres, lay close behind the German front and also that, because the sector had long been quiet, the Germans had constructed formidable defences in the Somme chalk, including dug-outs up to 40 feet below ground.' Originally the attack was to have had a larger French contribution, but, between February and June, the demands of Verdun meant that only 11 French divisions would be available for the offensive. Now for the first time in the war the British would be playing the leading role in an Allied offensive on the Western Front.

Christmas 1915 was a far more serious time than the previous year, although the presents and cards arrived from home, trees appeared in dugouts and Christmas meals were prepared. Last Christmas had been peaceful and troops had been able to go rearward for church services, but this year there was patrol activity up and down the line, and one regiment spent the Christmas period planning and practising for a major trench raid in order to take prisoners.

From the arrival of the war on the Somme, to the German withdrawal in early 1917, Serre was always in the front line. An August 1915 photograph showing the destruction caused by French artillery.

This happened on 29 December and was extremely successful.

By the end of the year, total German losses since August 1914 were 2,597,052, of which 601,751 were dead and 242,347 missing, presumed killed. However, despite the cost, Germany's military balance looked better than that of the Allies who had been frustrated at every turn by strong German defence in the west and the failure of the Italians in the south and the Russians in the east.

Relationships between the French and Germans was not always strained. Taken in the spring of 1915, a German soldier gives a ride to a local, watched by the young males of the village who could have been in the employ of the occupiers.

Looking back at Thiepval from the front line sometime in the summer of 1915.

Although shelled by the French for five months, Thiepval was still habitable and inhabited. The top picture shows the church and village centre. The bottom picture, taken from the church tower shows the damage to Thiepval Château

A transport wagon passing through Le Transloy in the autumn of 1915 when there was still enough feed for the horses to keep them in prime condition.

Both the French and Germans used mass graves to bury the dead, sometimes together on the battlefield where they fell. The third mass grave was in the village cemetery at Le Transloy where 676 French and 34 German soldiers were interred after the August 1914 fighting.

A rear communication trench on the western side of Le Transloy showing Gueudecourt on the left and another testimony to the strength of the fighting in the area during August and September 1914 – another French mass grave.

Newly arrived troops learning their way around in a training exercise.

In order to make sure of sufficient meat supplies, many of the Corps' set up slaughter houses with their own cattle farms to provide the animals. This herd was kept at Ligny during the summer of 1915 for the consumption of a reserve corps.

Even with an occupation, farmers continued to tend their fields using any available labour. Here women and older men thresh the 1915 harvest.

Troops out of the line needed rest, relaxation, food and exercise. A favoured sport during the summer months was the tug of war.

Troops making charcoal in a copse near Grévillers in August 1915.

Farmers on the Somme had long used oxen as draught animals, so, when their horses were commandeered by the German Army, they were still able to carry on with their jobs.

As supplies of all descriptions from the homeland became more difficult to procure, much use was made of captured materiel. Taken in Bapaume during 1915, this photo shows a Serbian cart being pulled by Russian horses.

With most transport reliant on horses, blacksmiths were very important members of the army. This group were responsible for shoeing the horses of a light ammunition column stationed at Grandcourt near Miraumont.

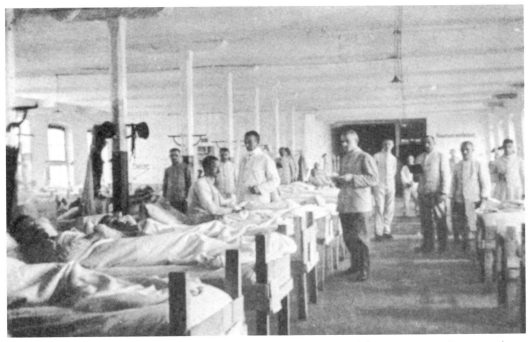

Any large building could be made into a hospital – a converted factory somewhere on the Somme in use as a Feldlazarett (Field Hospital) during 1915.

An impromptu concert in Flers held on 17 August 1915. Two soldiers areentertaining their comrades with a violin and a homemade zither.

War or no war, the seasons rolled on. Here in early summer, flowering herbs are collected for medicinal use.

As the war settled down to a routine, base units arrived behind the front to provide services for the front-line soldier out on rest. One important piece of equipment was the steam disinfection unit. This one was in a Field Hospital but others were maintained in areas where troops were sent to rest.

As Field Hospitals became fully established, they might install more advanced equipment, such as bacteriological pathology facilities.

Clothing, after steam disinfection, stored in a Field Hospital awaiting collection by their owners.

As well as setting up their own slaughterhouses and farms, many Infantry Corps set up their own dairies. This one is using both military and civilian personnel to produce butter.

Places of worship were installed in any suitable building, just as hospitals were. Here, a barn is used for a religious service in Flers on 27 January 1915.

During the summer months the vegetation provided extra cover for movement during the day. This photo, taken in June 1915, shows a ration party on their way to the front using a communication trench that started in a cultivated field. The troops are wearing fatigue jackets.

Among the season's greetings for many families would arrive news of the death of a loved one. Johann Mühlhauser, a twenty year old soldier in *12 Bavarian Infantry Regiment*, died a hero's death on 11 December.

Zum frommen Andenken im Gebete
an den tugendsamen Jüngling

Johann Mühlhauser,
Eckstetterbauerssohn von Wald,
Pfarrei Wang,

The inside and outside of a corps book shop. Each corps had its own printing and publications sections, attached to headquarters, for producing military publications and also books for purchase by the troops. Here two of the corps printing staff are pictured with the publications produced by their book printing section for sale to the soldiers.

Weihnachten 1915

Christmas 1915 in the officer's mess – a time for giving and enjoyment with a brief cessation from the war's hostilities; a year when there were still good things readily available.

The conditions in the trenches encouraged the spread of lice and the diseases they carried. Here, soldiers garrisoned at Serre wait their turn for inoculation against typhus in September 1915.

Chapter Three

1916

The start of the year saw the German troops living in better conditions than at the beginning of 1915, due to the improvements made that year. These included heating in dugouts and a regular supply of fuel so they could at least stay warm. Provisions were better - when they could be delivered - with divisions having set up their own bakeries, butchers, water bottling plants and slaughterhouses. However, no amount of work could change the weather; it was muddy like the previous year, making movement difficult at the very least. While, due to the improvements, most frontline dugouts were warm and dry, some were

The village of Flers in January 1916 showing a winter landscape and the muddy conditions developing on the roads.

Falkenhayn, Commander in Chief on the Western Front, wanted every yard of territory to be held to the last drop of blood. This cost the German Army some of its best soldiers.

not; some units during their week in the line never got out of wet boots or clothing. The improvements also meant more maintenance, as there were now three trench lines to maintain.

Early in 1916 the British took over from Arras south to the positions they held on the Somme to create a continuous British front. 'The Germans were alerted to the presence of these newcomers by the white puffs of their high-bursting shrapnel…and the unwelcome increase in the numbers of the enemy machine guns. The leisurely tic-tack of the French machine guns, which ceased after every twenty-five rounds to allow a new strip to be inserted, was replaced by the head-long and endless chatter of the new weapons, which sprayed our landscape with bullets and endangered our approach routes by night' wrote one soldier after the war.

There was also a general increase in activity after the British arrived. With Haig replacing French, Rupprecht noted a great deal more activity by the British infantry. Between January and the start of the offensive, British troops conducted 106 trench raids with a further 310 during the offensive. Trench raids, as the censor's inspection of letters showed, had a negative effect on German morale, especially on soldiers in reserve units from industrial areas. Crown Prince

Friedrich Weishaar, who was training to be a priest when the war broke out, was killed near Gommécourt, on 1 July 1916, while serving as a Gefreiter with *170 Infantry Regiment*.

Johann Langlechner, a thirty-three old farmer from Schönberg, died a hero's death during an artillery barrage on 29 August 1916 after serving for two years at the front.

Johann Langlechner.

Rupprecht noted in a letter sent home by such a soldier: 'the British are treating our men like children. One evening not long ago they betook themselves with their lethal clubs as far as the third trench, and proceeded to knock a number of men down and drag them off. The rest of our men ran for their lives! They were back here again yesterday. They caught the sentry crouching in a dugout and beat

Zum frommen Andenken im Gebete

an den ehrengeachteten Jüngling

Herrn Johann Thaler,

Hauptlehrerssohn von Würding,

Kanzleigehilfe beim k. Straßen- und Flußbauamt Simbach,

welcher als Kriegsfreiwilliger und Gefreiter in den Kämpfen an der Somme am 26. September 1916 im Alter von $19\frac{1}{2}$ Jahren nach 2jährigem Kriegsdienst den Heldentod fürs Vaterland gefunden hat.

Er ruhe in Frieden!

Ehre seinem Andenken!

Jesus, Maria, Joseph! (7 Jahre und 7 Quadr. Ablaß.) Pius X., 16. VI. 1906

Man bittet, diesen Ablaß dem teuern Verstorbenen zuzuwenden.

Zu beziehen bei J. Leeb, Würding.

Auf fremder Erde schlummerst Du,
Von fremder Hand gebracht zur Ruh:
Bitter, ach, ist unser Schmerz!
Doch unser Aug' schaut himmelwärts,
Wo Du nun weilst in ewiger Wonne,
Geschmückt mit einer Heldenkrone.
Denn die für Herd und Heimat sterben,
Vom Herrn als Lohn die Krone erben.

Gefreiter Johann Thaler, a nineteen year old war volunteer, was killed on 26 September 1916

him on the behind. They clubbed down several of our troops and took them prisoner.'

However, it was not always the British who had the upper hand. The Germans had spent a considerable amount of time honing their patrolling and raiding skills, and pulled off some spectacularly successful raids, one of which was against 2 South Wales Borderers of 29 Division. They had been in the line for only three days when they were hit extremely hard and, as a result of the raid, the division suffered 112 casualties, with one officer and thirty three other ranks killed, eight officers and forty two men wounded, plus nineteen captured and nine men missing. The casualties sustained by the attacking regiment, as a result of the operation being planned and executed in line with the latest practice, were three killed and one seriously wounded. A retaliation attack a few days later, which the German defenders knew was coming from the activity that was easily observed, was brought 'to a standstill with pre-arranged artillery and small-arms fire as soon as it was launched.'

The German Army on the Western front was more skilled and better equipped for trench warfare than either of its opponents. It contained the survivors from the Allied offensives the previous year, men who had gained considerable experience and who were generally well led and resolute. It was strong in defence, as the British would find out when they attacked on the Somme on 1 July. Here the defences had been strengthened after the French assaults of 1915; its trench systems bristled with barbed wire, strong points, deep and spacious dugouts and

Bel Frommelles gefangene Engl.
auf dem Marsch durch Haubourdin. 20.7.16.

British POWs captured near Fromelles being marched through Haubourdin on 20 July 1916.

fortified villages – an awesome array of defensive measures to blunt the British attack.

German divisions were assigned to a specific sector of the front, and stayed put, they enjoyed the further advantage of an intimate knowledge of their area and its terrain as well as knowing the tactics they would use against any attackers. As soldier Max Heinz recalled: 'again and again we looked upon the same scene. We knew every house and every tree; at every turn of the way we knew just how far we were from our goal.'

When, by late April, no Allied relief operation had been launched to help the French who were fighting a bitter battle of attrition at Verdun, *OHL* became anxious as to where it would fall. General Fritz von Below, commander of *Second Army*, that was holding the positions between Noyon and Gommecourt, felt that the assault would come on this front, a sector held by only three Corps of 150,000 men and virtually no reserves. Too occupied with Verdun, Falkenhayn sent Labour Corps soldiers to construct third line positions and a detachment of captured Russian howitzers with little ammunition.

'There was feverish development of the positions...especially the Grallsburg and Schwaben redoubt.' The latter, being 'a point of defensive importance', the loss of which would endanger the southern bank of the Ancre, and provide the enemy with a view of the German artillery positions, was therefore well

Thirty-four year old Unteroffizier Paul Huber, Iron Cross 2nd Class, was serving with *I Artillery Munitions Column*, when he was killed on 2 July 1916.

British POWs take a break during their march to captivity along the road to Péronne.

Die große Schlacht im Westen.
An der Strasse nach Peronne rastende gefangene Engländer.

A shot-down British aircraft being inspected by German troops in early July.

constructed and manned by troops who knew its importance. The redoubt 'provided battle positions for three machine guns and four heavy automatic rifles, with a two man crew' and had a searchlight position and a signalling station, and, as building materials became 'available in quantity, the more elaborate the defences became.'

Aware that the British were planning something in the sector lent urgency to the improvements but even so, the work still had to be of a high standard. The changes were many: concrete squads built observation posts; church bells, sirens and gongs were installed to warn of gas attack; mine galleries were extended and wire defences strengthened; the number of telephone intercept stations increased, while their own telephone security was carefully regulated. To prevent the destruction of stores by British artillery, these were moved out of range and any civilians still living in the area were also moved back to safety. In order to improve ammunition supplies, shell proof dumps were built as far forward as the frontline.

By the end of April, the British had got the measure of German raiding tactics and started to turn them against the attackers, with occasional success. For example, on 24 April after *1 Battalion 99 Regiment* had taken over the trenches from *3 Battalion,* there was a sudden artillery barrage landed on the position. The

British troops cut the wire and succeeded in taking thirteen prisoners, but a repeat of the action nearly a week later was beaten off.

The increasing number of British troops meant that there had to be an increase in trench raids in order to gain unit identification. At the end of May, Hauptmann Wagener was ordered, at all costs, to bring in some prisoners. A 200 man strong raid was mounted at 0300 hours on 4 June. It failed, with the loss of twenty men killed or injured, and one soldier being taken prisoner by the British! Leading a second attack that evening, Hauptmann Wagener and his men captured seventeen British soldiers.

Even with the accumulated evidence Falkenhayn did not agree with von Below, still believing that it was not the Somme but the Scarpe that be the area for the Allied offensive. General von Below was so confident that the attack would be on his sector that he asked permission to launch a spoiling attack to halt the Allied preparations; the Russian offensive put a halt to any such plans.

That the offensive was coming was corroborated by espionage and by a British government minister who commented that munitions workers were postponing their holidays until the end of June; very quickly it was public knowledge across Europe. Rupprecht, commander of *Sixth Army*, in the area Falkenhayn thought would bear the brunt of the attack, came to the same conclusion as von Below: it would a joint British and French assault north and south of the Somme. This

The main street in Combles before the British attack.

Christliches Andenken
an den ehrengeachteten Jüngling
Alois Weber
Wagner in Hainstetten,
beim k. b. Pionier-Regt., 2. Res.-Komp.
welcher nach 15monatlicher treuer
Pflichterfüllung im Alter von 25 Jahren
in den heißen Kämpfen an der Somme
am 3. Oktober 1916 nachts 1 Uhr, an
den Folgen eines Granatschusses, den
Heldentod fürs Vaterland gefunden hat.

Druck von J. Nothhaft, Deggendorf.

Alois Weber, a twenty-five year old soldier, serving with *6 Pioneer Regiment*, was killed in action on 3 October 1916 during an artillery barrage.

Twenty-one year old Private Ludwig Danninger, serving with *20 Bavarian Infantry Regiment*, died of his wounds on 7 November 1916.

Ehre dem Andenken
des tugendsamen Jünglings
Hrn. Ludwig Danninger
Oekonomensohn von Danning
bei Kirn,
Soldat beim kgl. bayer. 20. Inf.-Regt.,
welcher an der S.... schwer verwundet
und am 7. November 1916 im Lazarett
in Zastrop im 21. Lebensjahre den Heldentod für's Vaterland gestorben ist.

Abschied von Mutter und Geschwistern
Nahmst du auf ein Nimmerwiederseh'n,
Und uns der Mutter und Geschwistern
Wollt' ob dem Schmerz das Herz vergeh'n.
Schwer ist der Schlag, der uns getroffen,
Zerrissen ist das zarte Band. —
Doch süßer Trost ist uns geblieben:
Du starbst als Held für's Vaterland!

Zu haben bei Scheipl in Kirn.

was confirmed by the arrival of French troops in British positions; the Germans initially thought these were there for defence when the British attacked, but trench raids soon discovered that the new troops were from XX Corps, a unit known as an excellent offensive formation.

Regardless of this information, German headquarters did not believe that the French, due to their commitments at Verdun, would be a major force in the coming battle, and weakened their defences in the French zone by moving *10 Bavarian Division* to the British sector. During the reorganisation needed to deal with the loss of a division, French artillery shelling increased, interfering with the relocation of the remaining units. The reserve division, *2 Garde Reserve,* was also put into the line, near Gommecourt, because the attack was expected in the northern sector.

Like their enemy, the British were also keen to probe to find who they were

Ludwig Pess, a twenty year old theological student, was killed during an artillery barrage on 1 November 1916.

Private Georg Friedl, a twenty-five year old soldier from Hallwang, died on 10 August from wounds sustained on 22 July, while serving with *18 Bavarian Infantry Regiment.*

Alois Schreiner, a thirty-eight year old farmer's son fom Deglberg, serving with *10 Reserve Infantry Regiment,* died on 18 August 1916.

Peter Weiss, a twenty-four year old farmer's son from Gailberg, serving in *19 Bavarian Infantry Regiment*, died on 24 September in Field Hospital 89, from wounds sustained on 9 September 1916.

facing, how alert they were, and how strong their response to attack would be. Trench raiding was also felt to be important in maintaining and improving the offensive spirit of otherwise static troops. Having learned from the Germans, no dead would provide any form of identification because all identification marks were left behind before the raid. On 6 June, after a concentrated artillery attack, a strong British patrol forced its way into infantry position C8, capturing a junior NCO and ten men. The simultaneous attacks on either flank resulted in the capture of men from *Reserve Infantry Regiment 110,* but *Reserve Infantry Regiment 119* successfully pushed the attackers back without a prisoner.

All the signs pointed to a major offensive in the very near future. Final preparations were made, and headquarters staff moved into their allotted battle positions; the defenders settled down and waited. On the night of 23/24 June, a raiding party in the Gommecourt sector captured a prisoner who confirmed both the attack day and place. Using open-ended questioning techniques that encouraged captives to speak more freely while still in shock from combat and capture, German intelligence officers, who were more systematic than British ones, got the soldier to tell them that the attack would be on a thirty-mile front, five days after the artillery barrage had started on 26 June. Even when the barrage started, on villages kilometres to the rear, where till then life had continued almost normally, as the shells rained down, killing and wounding soldier and civilian alike, Falkenhayn was still not convinced that this was real, and left only three divisions as its immediate reserve.

With the British artillery pounding villages well behind the front line, those civilians who were left had to be rapidly evacuated with only what they could carry - a process happening along the entire Somme front. At Longueval, when the artillery fire increased, the local population were told to make ready for almost immediate evacuation – three hours in which to be ready. Carrying what they could, they walked to the loading point, knowing that they would return to

A humorous photo with dog over nose cone taken in July 1916 – a charitable gift for Bapaume from the English.

A view of the ever-growing soldiers' cemetery at Ablainzeville taken in August 1916 by Hauptmann Hammersen.

desolation. A large wagon arrived to transport the elderly, lame, sick and the children, but was quickly taken over by the rich with the permission of the mayor. Vizefeldwebel Weickel, whose job it was to supervise the process, was forced to intervene, and summarily removed those who were capable of walking, giving their places to those for whom they were intended.

A further advantage enjoyed by the defenders was their geographical position: the attack area was a rolling chalk plain, the surface of which was a mixture of sand, silt and clayey loam, now where very deep; underneath was chalk that provided excellent dugouts and trenches. With the highest points being no more than 150 feet, the ridges assumed great importance to both sides for the field of view and fire they provided. In the north and centre of the assault area the Germans held the higher ground, allowing them to see down the Ancre valley beyond Albert, but in the south the situation was generally reversed. However, some of the woodlands so hotly contested during the battle gave the German troops cover from view.

However, it was not always necessary to hold the high ground to gain a good view. British aircraft flew over the German lines taking photographs, dropping bombs and radioing back troop positions to their artillery. These real-time transmissions and responses gave the Germans little warning unless the message was intercepted and translated in time.

A view of the church and village pond in Achiet-le-Petit taken in September 1916, showing that some places still remained untouched by war.

Soldiers' graves in a wood at Achiet-le-Petit, photographed by Gefreiter Pförtner.

As the bombardment increased in intensity, casualties mounted and more damage was done to the trenches. Each night these would be repaired as far as possible, only to be blown away the next morning; in some places the trenches were replaced by a series of shell holes. However, the deeper dugouts were relatively undamaged and, when the shelling stopped, the occupants rushed to the parapet, in most cases getting there before the British, to the cost of the latter. Forewarned, the troops knew what to expect - a full-scale attack, as did General von Below. He expressed his concerns in his evening report for 28 June: 'enemy activity resembles (the) tactics of wearing down and attrition. It must be assumed that the bombardment…will continue for some time…The enormous enemy superiority in heavy and long-range batteries, which our army has so far been unable to counter, is proving very painful…our infantry is suffering heavy losses day after day, whilst the enemy is able to preserve his manpower.' He also expressed concern about the number of infantry he was opposing and the fact that the German artillery could not touch them.

The French themselves provided further support for an attack south of the river, in the French sector. On the night of 27 June, an assault designed to test

Loading an infantry battalion on to trucks, ready to return to the front line after a rest in the peaceful village of Achiet-le-Grand. Photo taken by Gefreiter Meyer in August 1916.

The quiet village of Ayette, in the backwaters of the Somme, taken on 28 October 1916 by Gefreiter Glaser.

the strength of the positions held by *Infantry Regiment 60* was launched after 'a storm of small arms fire.' With the flares being released and the artillery response, the sky was like day, clearly highlighting the advancing troops who quickly returned to their own lines under the withering German response. The next evening the French returned, getting closer but not succeeding in getting into the position.

'It was Haig's intention that Rawlinson's Fourth Army - created on 1 March - should take the German front defences from Serre to Montauban, followed by the German second position from Pozières to the Ancre and the slopes in front of Miraumont on the first day.' On the northern flank 46 and 56 Divisions would attempt to pinch out the German salient at Gommecourt in a diversionary operation. To their right, 31, 4 and 29 Divisions (VIII Corps) would attack between Beaumont Hamel and Serre. On the other side of the Ancre, 36 (Ulster) and 32 Divisions (X Corps) were to assault the Thiepval defences, including the daunting Schwaben and Leipzig Redoubts. 8 and 34 Divisions (III Corps) would attack Ovillers and La Boisselle, astride the Albert-Bapaume road. XV Corps, comprising 21, 17 and 7 Divisions, was to secure Fricourt and Mametz; and on the right, next to the French, 18 and 30 Divisions (XIII Corps) would capture Montauban. North and south of the River Somme itself, General Fayolle's French Sixth Army would assist the British advance by attacking towards the German second position

With the Allied offensive forthcoming, the remaining civilians were evacuated. Here, their possessions loaded in a wagon, they are passing through Bapaume on their way to a quieter area.

Entertaining the remaining civilians in June 1916. Leutnant Kuhlmann's photograph shows a regimental band performing in the town square in Bapaume.

The results of the British shelling of Bapaume – the exit to Péronne pictured during November 1916.

opposite Péronne, between Maurepas and Flaucourt. Should the initial assault gain its objectives, Haig aimed to burst through the German second position on the higher ground between Pozières and Ginchy and, in due course, capture the third position in the Le Sars-Flers sector, thus threatening Bapaume. This might, in turn, clear the way for the Reserve Army, formed on 23 May, to swing northwards, in the direction of Arras.'

Evidence from the military attaché in Madrid, and reports in French newspapers, confirmed the date, and the capture of another British soldier who knew of the attack convinced OHL that the attack was imminent. Numerous British soldiers were captured during this period and interrogations provided the date, time and extent, but an exact picture was not possible, because the attack after a five-day bombardment should have been launched on 29 June, but was postponed on 28 June until 1 July.

However, the cost before the assault began had been destructive and expensive in lives. Much of the front and second line positions had been demolished and the defenders had incurred over 10,000 casualties. 'The preliminary bombardment had had a significant physical and psychological effect, rendering much of the defensive sector untenable. In most places it was only the uncut wire and the plodding nature of the British advance that provided the opportunity and time for the German machine gunners to recover from their ordeal.'

There was little surprise left when on 30 June a listening post intercepted a message from British Fourth Army wishing all ranks good luck for the attack on 1 July. Only the time of the attack was still unknown and when a mine was exploded ten minutes before the start time the whole game had been given away. In the trenches some men prayed, others cursed the British for the dire situation they were in but most just wanted it happen: 'Oh God, free us from this ordeal; give us release through battle, grant us victory.'

At 0820 hours German time, on a perfect summer's day, a mine exploded under the men of *9 Company Reserve Infantry Regiment 119* who were manning trenches on Hawthorn Ridge. The debris blocked dugout entrances, delaying the response of many of the German defenders; soon, though, 'a pitched battle for possession of the crater and its surroundings was in full flow.' On the Allied side, men shook hands, prayed and prepared themselves for the coming attack, and, at 0730 hours, they rose from their trenches in their tens of thousands and moved into no man's land.

M. Gerster in his book "Die Schwaben an der Ancre", described the wait and the attack of 8 British Division around Ovillers. Everyone knew that the intense bombardment was a prelude to an attack, so 'the men in the dug-outs…waited ready, belts full of hand-grenades around them, gripping their rifles and listening

The remains of Bapaume church in November 1916, after being hit by British heavy artillery shells.

2 July and a heavy artillery shell lands on the Bapaume to Douai road.

Bazentin church taken by Leutnant Roser, in April 1916 before the bombardment started.

Damage caused by the shelling of Bapaume during August 1916. Top – the town square, and (bottom) the road to Arras.

for the bombardment to lift…on to the rear defences. It was of vital importance to lose not a second in taking up position in the open to meet the British infantry which would advance immediately behind the artillery barrage. Looking towards the British trenches…through the long trench periscopes…there could be seen a mass of steel helmets above the parapet showing that the storm-troops were ready for the assault.'

The British troops had been led to believe that there would be few left alive after such a bombardment, but the defenders would quickly show them that they were wrong. 'At 7.30 A.M. the hurricane of shells ceased as suddenly as it had begun,' and, while the British climbed out of their trenches, the defenders climbed out of their dugouts and ran in small groups or singly to shell craters to wait for the attacking troops. Pulling their machine guns out of the dug-outs, dragging heavy ammunition boxes behind them, they rapidly set up a rough firing line and looked towards the British lines to see a series of extended lines of infantry moving towards them. 'The first line appeared to continue without end to right

Bringing up the stores. The German Army used a considerable amount of horse drawn transport because, compared to the Allied forces on the Western Front, it suffered from a lack of oil products. The photo was taken on the main street of Bucquoy in October 1916 by Leutnant Kuhlmann.

The road to Beaucourt sur l'Ancre from Beaumont Hamel at the end of October 1916, photographed by Gefreiter Pförtner.

Collecting fresh water from a spring at Beugnâtre during July 1916.

A well signposted tree in the centre of Beugnâtre, giving directions to units, facilities and the nearby villages, pictured by Rittmeister Neunhoeffer in August 1916.

As it was some distance behind the lines, Bucquoy was a rest area. Here soldiers pose for Gefreiter Pförtner outside the artist's house.

and left. It was quickly followed by a second line, then a third and fourth. They came on at a steady pace as if expecting to find nothing alive in our trenches. Some appeared to be carrying kodaks (in reality pigeon baskets, power buzzers or other experimental equipment) to perpetuate the memory of their triumphal march across the German defences.'

As the attackers reached halfway, the order to get ready was given. The defenders made final adjustments and then, when the British troops were within 100 yards, 'the rattle of machine-gun and rifle fire broke out along the whole line of shell-holes. Some fired kneeling so as to get a better target…whilst others, in the excitement of the moment, stood up regardless of their own safety, to fire into the crowd of men in front of them.' And then, in response to the red rockets the artillery joined the fight, firing shells that burst amongst the advancing troops. 'Whole sections seemed to fall, and the rear formations, moving in closer order, quickly scattered. The advance rapidly crumpled under this hail of shell and bullets. All along the line men could be seen throwing up their arms and collapsing, never to move again. Badly wounded rolled about in their agony, and others, less severely injured, crawled to the nearest shell hole for shelter.'

In other places the story was similar, but different. At Gommecourt, a British prisoner had provided the defenders with complete details of what to expect and, while the bombardment had done severe damage to trenches and wire, most of the dugouts had survived, allowing local counterattacks to quickly restore the

The memorial stone in Bucquoy cemete[r] honouring the dead of a Reserve Infantr[y] Regiment. Photograph taken in Novemb[er] 1916 by Gefreiter Meyer.

The main street in Boursies, well behind the front, in September 1916. Military transport is horse drawn, all the horses having been commandeered from civilia[n] while local transport relies on a draught

November 1916 in Crèvecouer-sur-l'Escaut. French POWs with a mounted escort waiting to take them to the station for transport to Germany.

Combles was little affected by the war until July 1916. This is the village church in February 1916 taken by Hauptmann Weber.

A quiet village a safe distance back from the front, Combles provided some respite from the daily worries of the trenches. One of its attractions was a cinema, this one run by 12 Infantry Division, a unit that suffered heavily during the 1916 battles.

The château at Contalmaison pictured on 28 June 1916 by Major Gericke. With three days to go before the attack, long-range heavy artillery has already taken its toll on the fine building.

situation in the newly-entered front line trenches. In the southern sector, where again, the British entered the front line trenches and then the second line, there was stiff resistance and by the end of the day the attack had been repulsed. By the end of the day in the Gommecourt sector, *Reserve Infantry Regiment 55* and *91* counted over 2,500 dead British soldiers for the loss of three officers and 182 men.

To the south at Serre, the losses were equally staggering. In 1915 the area had been hotly contested with the French because it occupied vital high ground that controlled the defence of the line north of the River Ancre. Between then and the start of the Somme offensive, considerable effort had turned the area into a virtually impregnable fortress. *169 Infantry Regiment* in position at Serre watched the 'Pals Battalions' advance. Using their rifles and machine guns to the utmost, 'wild firing slammed into the masses of the enemy...barrels are changed...the barrel must be changed again. It's red hot and the cooling water is boiling – the hands working the weapon are scorched and burned – "Keep firing!"...or shoot

The main street in Courcelette pictured during July 1916 by Gefreiter Meyer.

yourself"…the enemy closes up…we fire endlessly…the British keep charging forward. Despite the fact that hundreds are already lying dead in the shell holes…fresh waves keep emerging. We have got to fire…skin hangs in ribbons from the fingers of the burnt hands of the gunners…the youth of England bled to death in front of Serre.'

According to German divisional and regimental histories, apart from Hawthorn Crater and Heidenkopf (Quadrilateral) Redoubt, there were no real penetrations by the attacking force, but troops from the 31 British Division did take and hold part of the front line until driven out, losing thirty-four prisoners. The 4, 29 and 31 British Divisions had faced three defending regiments whose total casualties amounted to just over 1,200 whilst their casualties were a staggering 14,000 killed, wounded, missing and POW. In total, four front-line divisions had taken on twelve British divisions between Gommecourt and Montauban and apart from *12 Division* that had been driven from its trenches by 18 and 30 British Divisions, held their positions and won the day.

Heidenkopf had been bypassed and it was only when British troops moved back that it was occupied by them. Later in the morning, a counterattack started to push the British slowly back and, after heavy fighting, the position was retaken by the end of the day. Some British troops made it back to their lines, leaving a few to be taken prisoner; a search in the craters in front of Heidenkopf, the next day, resulted in the capture of more British soldiers – in total 200 men were captured. Discarded equipment and British and German corpses were everywhere. While *Reserve Infantry Regiment 121* had 151 men killed, they counted over 1700 British dead in front of their lines.

The story was repeated elsewhere along the British line, but it was not the same story south of the River Somme. Further south, to the consternation of *OHL*, the

A photo taken by Leutnant Müller in Courcelles-le-Comte during August 1916 of veterans of the Somme battles, resting well behind the lines, and finding time to enjoy themselves.

Behind the lines life continued as normal during the summer of 1916, but even a village well behind the front had a sentry box in the village square.

Rustic house at Courcelette still inhabited by a local family on 14 June 1916, when the photo was taken by Gefreiter Haberecht. When the Allied artillery barrage started, the inhabitants were moved to a safer area well behind the front.

There was rarely time to bury the dead individually during the initial phases of the war. Leutnant Aurin took this photo of an October 1914 mass grave on the outskirts of Courcelles-le-Comte. Unusually this is a mass grave for 141 French and 29 German soldiers.

Courcelles-le-Comte in July 1916. Rested troops boarding transport for the return to the front.

Ervillers, a country town on the road to Arras, pictured in July 1916 by Hauptmann Hammersen.

French, who they thought were too occupied at Verdun to have any spare capacity, also mounted an offensive and had achieved most of their objectives. The importance of the lost ground and artillery pieces is clearly shown by the sending of fifteen heavy batteries from Verdun to assist the Somme defenders.

French intentions had been completely misread. Defending units were over-stretched along the frontage they held and had been effectively shelled by the French artillery, which had destroyed or suppressed many artillery emplacements, as well as burying or destroying many machine guns and mortars; gas shells had also been used extensively before the attack to reduce the effectiveness of the German artillery.

It was not a good day for the German Army in the southern sector when, in a mist, the French attacked two hours after the British. The attack was not expected; any artillery support that might have helped the defending infantry was quickly neutralised by the French using very low-flying spotting aircraft and manned balloons to quickly and accurately determine the positions of the German batteries. Opposite the French XX Corps, nearly all the deep dugouts in the first line were blown in, and only a few of the very deep ones were still partly useable, leaving most of the garrison lying in mine and shell craters. Under the protection of the thick morning mist, the front line was quickly overrun.

While the French employed ten heavy batteries for each kilometre of the attack, there was an almost total lack on the German side so that little counter-battery work could be undertaken. As a result the villages of Becquincourt, Dompierre and Frise fell quickly to the attackers. By midday, German artillery was virtually silent

Further south in the French attack zone, troops had reached Fay, while the line between Assevilers and Herbécourt – of almost 2 ½ kilometres - was being hard pressed, defended by over-extended units. By 1600 hours, the former had fallen and, at 1730 hours, the latter was attacked and taken. After a vigorous counter-attack, it was retaken by hand-to-hand fighting, from the Senegalese troops who were still prepared to continue to fight from it, even when wounded or taken prisoner, using their concealed weapons. By the evening, the French Sixth Army had reached all its objectives, gone beyond them at certain points, and engaged the German second position; casualties had been light, no reserves had been needed and more than 4,000 prisoners had been taken, half of these had been captured by the Colonial Corps.

As the day drew to a close, fighting continued into the night in some areas. Where the attack had failed completely and it was obvious that surviving attackers posed no threat, unofficial truces occurred and the defenders, in some cases, helped the British wounded: 'In front of our divisional sector lie the British in companies, in battalions: mowed down in rows…From No Man's Land…comes one great groan. The battle dies away…First aid men hasten around the area. A

As the battle lines moved east, villages like Ervillers had to be evacuated. Pictured on 25 September 1916, the villagers are being provided with transport to a safer area.

Underground in a bombardment proof shelter at Gommécourt in October 1916, machine gun troops fill ammunition belts before returning to duty in the trenches.

Flers, some distance behind the line, was used as a resting area for units on rotation from the front. This photo, taken in Spring 1916 by Oberarzt Harling, shows one of the village houses that has been turned into a reading room.

Another photo by Oberarzt Harling showing the soldiers' cemetery and memorial in Flers not long before the start of the offensive.

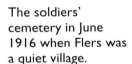

The soldiers' cemetery in June 1916 when Flers was a quiet village.

complete British medical team with stretcher bearers and unfurled Red Cross flags appears from somewhere…Where to begin? Whimpering and moaning confronts them from almost every square metre. Our own first aiders, who are not required elsewhere, go forward to bandage the wounded and deliver the enemy carefully to their own people.'

In the afternoon, with the attack well under way, *OHL* sent three divisions to support, not *Second Army* that was fighting the British, but the *Sixth Army* around Arras, where Falkenhayn thought the real attack would come. Even after nearly three days of the Somme battle, Falkenhayn was still of the opinion that *Sixth Army* would bear the brunt of any British attack.

In the early morning of 2 July, a counterattack against Bernafay Wood was stopped by a shrapnel barrage from the British 30 Division artillery, who later tried to burn the wood with a thermite barrage; this first trial of a new weapon was unsuccessful. A British patrol entered Fricourt and the village was occupied shortly afterwards. More than 100 prisoners were taken. Further patrols occupied stretches of German trench, but, overall, there were no large scale attacks.

However, in the evening of 3 July, *OHL* confidently announced that the Anglo-French offensive on the Somme had been halted and in some places repulsed but each day the Allies continued their relentless attacks, constantly wearing down their opponents who did not have the reserves they had. But reinforcements did arrive and, by the time the British Fourth Army was ready to attack again in force, vital improvements to the German defensive line had been achieved.

Losses were mounting due to massive use of artillery by the British to destroy second line positions and, where dugouts were not deep enough, casualties were very heavy, with units reporting losses of over a third of the available manpower. The constant shelling and continued British attacks disrupted communications making large scale operations difficult to coordinate and making it difficult to relieve front line battalions. Further reinforcements were on the way, but the scale of the attack, and the numbers needed to counter it, affected the course of the war in other sectors; particularly Verdun where any response was to be defensive and was to remain defensive until the Somme situation had changed. By 11 July, Falkenhayn had realised the seriousness of the situation.

British POWs under escort through Frémicourt on their way to the rear. The photo was taken by Vizefeldwebel Watzke in July 1916.

Höhe 110, or King George's Hill (to the British) at Fricourt, when it was just a quiet grassy hill behind the front line, taken in May 1916 by Feldunterarzt Harlandt.

The divisional canteen at Gomiecourt, pictured in July 1916 by Hauptmann Thaler.

Before the battle started, the château at Gommécourt was already a ruin. Here soldiers pose in a shell crater for Gefreiter Pförtner during April 1916.

The success of the counterattacks was varied and in some places failed. There was no possibility of major counter moves because the Eingreif troops, assigned for this task had not arrived. Pressure from the French attack resulted in *XVII Korps* asking for and receiving permission to withdraw to a more solid defensive line. Falkenhayn in response decreed that: 'the first principle of position warfare must be to yield not one foot of ground, and if it is be lost, to retake it by immediate counter-attack, even to the use of the last man,' thus dooming thousands of experienced troops to death in desperate attempts to retake ground of little tactical importance. 'Where you fall, there you lie. No one can help you.' This insistence soon meant that the defenders 'were suffering far higher casualties than they had even at the height of the assaults on Verdun. During the offensive's first ten days alone, the *2nd Army* had lost 40,187, as compared to the 25,989 men lost during the first ten days of the Verdun battle.'

Two weeks after the opening day of the offensive, the British attacked again, just before dawn, after a short barrage. The attack was not expected and, as the British troops were already in no man's land when the barrage started, they took the defenders by surprise. Even though the attack took 6,000 yards of second line trench between Bazentin-le-Petit and Longueval and Mametz, Bernafay and Trônes Woods had all fallen, and the British were unable to consolidate their gains and expand on them due to poor communications, lack of reserves and the German recovery.

As the battles continued, the order to hold at all costs was robbing the Germany army of some of its best men, men whom the army was finding it difficult to replace, whereas the British seemed to have no shortage of men or materiel. Reinforcements and fresh units from other sectors were quickly disillusioned by the Allied superiority in air power and artillery and, by mid-August, units were beginning to give up ground and surrender, to escape the pounding they were receiving. This was not true of every company, as Lieutenant Jünger found out when he returned to duty after being hit by shrapnel. His company had been put back into the line on the day after he was wounded and 'suffered severe losses marching up and also during ten hours' drumfire. It was then attacked from all sides owing to the large gaps in the line...nearly the whole company had died fighting to the last', only a few survived to be taken prisoner and none returned to Combles.

Artillery defined the Somme battles, killing, maiming, wounding and destroying, and also sending men mad. Jünger described the effect of artillery on Combles towards the end of August. 'Heavy artillery had turned a peaceful little billeting

Gommécourt Park, pictured by Gefreiter Pförtner in early July 1916, where the London Division fought a diversionary battle to help take the pressure off the main thrust at Serre.

The village of Gommécourt pictured after the 1 July attack.

With the Allied offensive only two months away, behind the lines, in villages like Haplincourt, life continued as it had always done. This picture, taken in May 1916, by Unteroffizier Müller, shows the main street through Haplincourt, with the village pond in the foreground and the as yet undamaged church in the background.

town into a scene of desolation in the course of a day or two. Whole houses had been flattened by single direct hits or blown up so that the interiors of the rooms hung over the chaos like the scenes on a stage. A sickly scent of dead bodies rose from many of the ruins, for many civilians had been caught in the bombardment and buried beneath the wreckage of their homes. A little girl lay in a pool of blood on the threshold of one of the doorways.' While the village was not being shelled, positions close by were being shelled; the artillery never stopped. Then in the afternoon it returned to the village, increasing in intensity until 'there was nothing but one terrific tornado of noise.' From 1900 hours onwards, the area where Jünger was sheltering was shelled by 15cm guns every thirty seconds; fortunately for him and fellow soldiers many of them were duds that only made the house rock. At 2000 hours two direct hits brought the house next door down and then the shelling increased again. Between '9 and 10 the shelling was frantic. The earth rocked and the sky boiled like a gigantic cauldron…innumerable shells came howling and hurtling over us. Thick smoke, ominously lit up by Verey lights, veiled

As the war moved east, villages like Grévillers came under threat and were subject to bombardment. The two pictures show the successive damage sustained by the church in August and September.

A farmer's house and stables at Manancourt, in use by the army in June 1916.

everything. Head and ears ached violently, and we could only make ourselves understood by shouting a word at a time…the power of logical thought …seemed suspended. A N.C.O. of No. 3 platoon went mad.'

Summer turned into autumn, and the hell of the Somme, as post-war writers who had served there called it, continued unabated. Losses were high on both sides but the Allies were finding it easier to replace losses. German divisions became burned out and had insufficient time to rest before being sent back to the front, so that they did not always perform as well as they could. Thiepval was a case in point: when *4 Garde Division* replaced the burned out *16 Division* south from Thiepval to Mouquet Farm, the British did not realise why no counterattack was mounted against Leipzig salient. The reason was simple: it was their 'second tour on the Somme and their senior officers had pleaded in vain that they were still in no fit state to return because of the literally incessant battering by the British artillery.'

Further replacement problems were caused by the constant use of the Eingrief and Sturm troops. This resulted in a two-tier system in the German Army with units for defence and special units for attack, resulting in a disproportionate loss of the better soldiers.

There was no innovation in defence, making the response to an Allied attack predictable and easily routed by artillery fire. Then there was the problem of Allied aircraft that appeared to enjoy complete freedom to strafe and bomb from a low height, to spot for artillery and photograph what they liked. While both sides were suffering, on the Allied side of the wire lessons were being learned and applied,

A quiet village well behind the battle zone, St. Leger, pictured in October 1916 by Wachtmeister Semler, showed no signs of a war apart from the troops and ubiquitous signs painted on the buildings. The pictures show military traffic in the high street and a soldiers' book handling depot.

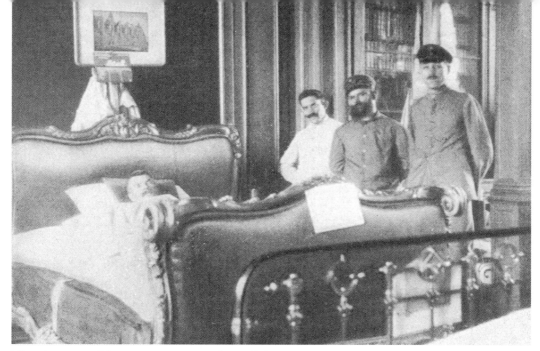

The château at Manancourt was used as a field hospital for the lightly wounded. This picture, taken in May 1916, shows a wounded officer in the previous owner's rather stately bed.

Taken in May 1916, by Unteroffizier Müller, this picture shows the well cared for soldiers' cemetery at Martinpuich.

The village street, clearly showing the church, taken in Miraumont in August 1916 by Gefreiter Meyer.

and a new weapon made its appearance – the tank; on the German side discipline and self-sacrifice were the watchwords.

Lieutenant Jünger amply described, with a hint of jealousy, the material wealth of his enemy and the strength of the RFC. 'At midday a man of my platoon got me to have a shot at a single Englishman in Guillemont railway station. When I looked I saw hundreds of English hurrying forward along a hallow communication trench. They were not particularly upset by the rifle-fire we could bring to bear on them. This sight showed the unequal terms on which we fought, for if we had ventured on anything like it our men would have been shot to pieces in a few minutes. While on our side not a captive balloon was to be seen, on the English side there were thirty at once over one spot, observing every movement with argus eyes and at once directing a hail of iron upon it.'

Then, on 29 August, Hindenburg and Ludendorff replaced Falkenhayn, and almost immediately changes in tactics and the Somme defences were planned.

However, things continued to get worse; losses for September were the worst for the whole offensive at 220,000 killed, wounded, missing or POW. As casualties mounted, replacement became ever harder, particularly when the Russians and Romanians assaulted Transylvania, the Italians launched the seventh Battle of the Isonzo River and the British attacked at Flers-Courcelette with tanks. As a result the troops spent longer in the line, had shorter rests, were given more to do - inevitably there was less chance of any counterattack being mounted.

However, some positions still held on eleven weeks after the start of the battle: Thiepval, on a commanding bluff, was part of the original first line attacked on 1 July. Its defenders had 'beaten off every attack on that day and every occasion since.' The fighting had been heavy around the position, leaving the countryside scarred and its slopes covered by debris – 'a litter beyond comparison of half - and quarter-buried men, with broken gear and dud shell and old bombs…helmets torn into spirals, gasmasks, rotten sandbags, bones, backbones, old legs, boots, old wheels, miles of bedevilled wire, packsacks…rifles, bayonets, bits of spines, tins, canteens, socks, gloves, and a litter of burst shells and a pox of shell-holes.'

The constant attrition fighting meant that reinforcements could come from anywhere, even the navy. In late September, naval soldiers who had been holding positions along the coast, north of Nieuwpoort and east of the Yser River, were moved to the Somme front. *Marine Infantry Regiments 1, 2* and *3* – the *Marine Infantry Brigade* – technically a division, relieved *8 Infantry Division*, in the Staufen Riegel after a couple of days' acclimatisation, during which they dug trenches. Coming from a quieter sector, the intensity of the shelling was new to them as were the troops they opposed – Canadians, who launched repeated attacks.

Lightly wounded troops from the battle were sent to convalescent centres just behind the front. This photo, taken in September 1916 by Gefreiter Schnelle, shows lightly wounded soldiers in front of the hospital tents at Morchies, a safe distance behind the front.

In most conquered villages there was a military cemetery and often a mass grave. Moislains soldiers' cemetery, pictured in June 1916, contained mass graves for French and German troops.

(Below) Lightly wounded troops waiting around the village pond at Morchies, to board vehicles to take them either back to their units, or further back from the front.

Morchies was an important centre for the lightly wounded from the Somme battlefields. Here, again pictured by Gefreiter Schnelle, in a different part of the village, are lightly wounded troops waiting to be returned as fit or for transit to other hospitals.

When they reached their positions, there was no trace of a trench. The dugouts were smashed or buried and all around lay discarded weapons and equipment; it was a completely new type of war to them. As they arrived, they found dead-tired troops who left their positions immediately. Even the commanding officer wanted to escape, though he was forced to remain behind to hand over. He explained rapidly that there were no real positions due to the constant bombardment, and, when it did stop, the 'Tommies' would attack. His only advice was to watch Kenora trench because that would be where the attack would begin. Handing over a sketch of the trench he left: 'I am delighted to be able to escape from this hell. Goodbye! Farewell!' As predicted, the next day the 'Tommies' attacked with wave after wave of Canadians assaulting their positions. There were severe losses on both sides. The Marines held their position and, with the coming of dark, the fighting ended.

By the end of September, a month that had cost the Germans nearly 135,000 casualties, many as POWs, the High Command began to doubt the powers of resistance of its men and found a reason: 'Hitherto our infantry had been inferior to that of the enemy in numerical terms, but in quality it had been superior. Now the heavy losses, and especially among the officers and NCOs, has reduced this qualitative advantage to a considerable degree.'

It was this situation that led to the decision to prepare the Siegfried Stellung, a much shorter and stronger trench system, some considerable distance behind the present front. A change in tactics would result in its defence being flexible and deep. Work began on planning the new defensive line in late September.

The French also continued to apply pressure on the German positions. One especially hotly-contested area was Sailly-Saillisel, where the French had pushed as far as the village church. The constant French attacks required repeated counter-attacks to push them back. While the artillery managed to disrupt the attackers, there was still continual and costly hand-to-hand fighting. However, despite the French drum fire on their positions and the continual attacks, the defenders held on.

With the constant attacks, the German artillery was often unclear where their own infantry were and frequently fired short, with devastating effect on their own men. One regiment reported that fifty percent of its casualties came from their own guns. Eventually the French pressure was too much, and Sailly-Saillisel fell to 152 Infantry Regiment.

Although the Allied artillery generally dominated the fighting, this was not always the case, as the French found out after their successful attack on 9 November. On that day, the British made a successful advance and the French broke into the trenches at Le Transloy. Although the territorial gain was small in

Entrance to the collection point for the lightly wounded soldier at Morchies in September 1916. The sign above the arch reads: Lightly wounded collection place for Army Group Stein.

This photograph by Gefreiter Schnelle shows the arrival of lightly wounded troops on 8 November.

Officers' mess in Mory pictured in August 1916 by Leutnant Becker.

Maid of Orléans statue in Péronne, pictured in June 1916 by Leutnant Wellensiek.

Vizefeldwebehl Schweizer photographed this communication trench near Pozières in April 1916.

Well behind the lines, the field hospital at Pronville in October 1916, photographed by Feld-Unterarzt Harlandt.

the French sector, it threatened Saillisel and St. Pierre Vaast Wood, ground the French needed to take to break through. With the French holding part of the wood, a counterattack was necessary. The assault time was set for 0448 hours on 15 November, after a long artillery barrage that would become drumfire from 0200 hours onwards. The shooting was extremely accurate with the shells landing on the trenches opposite the waiting assault troops. Just before the assault, French deserters jumped into the German trenches yelling for mercy. They could not endure the artillery any longer. At the appointed time, through bullets and shells, the German infantry rushed to the French front line to find its garrison dead. As the Germans threw grenades ahead of them, wounded French troops surrendered and marched off to the German lines. Pushing on they quickly took their objective as even more troops surrendered.

The attacks and counterattacks continued, the former with some success but rarely easily won. Many places were fought over many times, an example being the Butte de Warlencourt. Here the defenders were under orders to defend the Roman tumulus to the utmost; it afforded unobstructed views as far as Windmill Hill at Pozières, and the remains of Delville and High woods, allowing a more equal duel between German and British artillery. The ground around the butte was covered in dead British troops but it did not fall, even when a tank stumbled into the middle of an attack paralysising the defenders. The next day the South Africans attacked and likewise were eventually pushed back, leaving their dead. Even though it was the middle of autumn, the bodies decomposed quickly. Hans Pflugbeil wrote after he war: 'the masses of British dead in front our position were giving forth such a stench of corruption that our brave defenders could not touch their food.'

The battle of the Somme was not confined to the ground; there was also considerable activity above it. Initially the air advantage had been with the Allies but by October it was swinging towards the German air force. There were now over three hundred aircraft in the area including the new Albatross, superior in every respect to the best Allied planes. With more planes available, air battles naturally became bigger. Over the trenches occupied by *Reserve Infantry Regiment 76,* an air battle occurred with over fifty aircraft. The dogfight the ground troops were able to see was so quick and confused that they could barely identify their own planes. The ascendancy of the German air force had a reassuring effect on the ordinary soldier, who not only felt supported, but now worried less about the Allied planes and what they could see. And, with a more aggressive approach, they now took the war to the Allies in an attempt to demoralise them. They demonstrated their power by machine-gunning Allied positions whenever they could.

One pilot described aerial combat in late October. 'Over the smoking

Garrison troops arriving at Pronville during August 1916 photographed by Leutnant Kuhlmannn.

A roll call for horses, Sains-les-Marquion, in August 1916, before they were taken into the German Army.

May 1916 on the main street through Ruyalcourt. A company of infantry march through on their way to the front, photographed by Fahrer (driver) Braun.

Puisieux photographed in September 1916, showing the effects of the British bombardment.

desolation of shell craters, enemy and German air forces clashed. Real air battles developed. Aircraft fell like flaming torches to the ground. Whirling wings glittered in the sun. Here and there planes came down, landing luckily, or unluckily, after desperate attempts to control them. The enemy was forced back...into their own airspace.' The official despatch for 22 October stated that there had been over 500 sorties and 209 aerial battles with the enemy, which shot down sixteen enemy aircraft and damaged more.

The weather was wet, rifles were covered in mud and were starting to rust, and although the British advance towards Bapaume had been stopped, the battle was not over. After actions on the Ancre, at Beaumont Hamel and at Serre, the German High Command believed that they had survived the storm, giving Rupprecht time to go on leave to Bavaria. However, on 18 November when the first snow of the season was falling, the British attacked again with some success, and although the battle was over by the end of the day, a group of over 150 British soldiers, finding themselves cut off, went to ground in captured dugouts, taking prisoner any passing German 'until somebody noticed on 23 November. The Engländernest beat off two attacks the next day' but were finally captured by storm troops on 25 November.

'By the afternoon of 18 November the snow had been succeeded by rain which turned the ground into brown mud. The wet weather persisted over the following

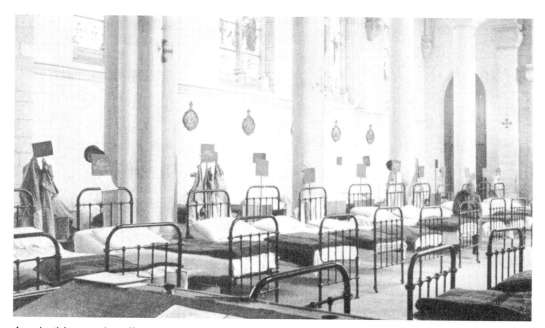

Any building with sufficient space was taken into use as a temporary hospital. This shows the church at Sains-les-Marquion in August 1916 ready to receive patients.

April 1916 – headstones in the soldiers' cemetery in Le Sars, with a wooden memorial in the background, all of unusual design.

days, and the Germans tried to cheer themselves up with the thought that "things must be just as bad for the Tommies"…It was a desolate consolation, and the continuing rain and the endless exhausting labour brought the morale and combat-worthiness…to the lowest ebb of the year.'

'As far as human judgement could foresee everything pointed to the Western Front as the scene of our chief defensive fighting in 1917' wrote Ludendorff in his memoirs. With that thought, changes had to be made to defence tactics. On 26 November instructions were issued to start work on the Siegfried Stellung.

On 17 December, Crown Prince Rupprecht, in a secret order congratulated the troops of the *First* and *Second* Armies for their courage during the battle of the Somme: 'the enemy sought to break through and attacked repeatedly…each attempt failed; the only gain being a narrow strip of utterly ruined terrain'. To the German Army it was a victory: 'the greatest battle of the war, perhaps the greatest of all time, has been won' he wrote to his troops. Although it might have been classed as a victory, General von Kuhl regarded the casualty rate as detrimental to the functioning of the army: 'the casualties suffered by Germany hit it harder

The main street through Vaulx-Vraucourt to Bapaume in June 1916 with troops moving to the front and empty supply wagons returning to base.

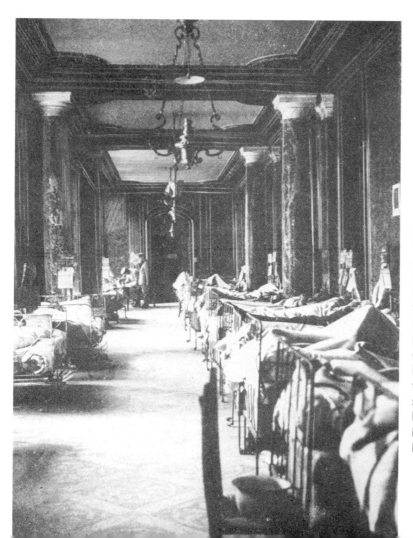

In England, Indian soldiers coming round in Brighton Pavilion thought they had gone to Heaven; for Germans this room must have provided a similar experience. A hospital ward – taken in July 1916 – showing the luxurious conditions in the Vélu château Field hospital.

A picturesque scene behind the lines at Villers-au-Flos taken in January 1916. Apart from the uniforms, everything appears to be as normal.

Life continued as far as possible to normal, even though there was an occupying force in the area. With few men left in the occupied zone behind the lines, women took over their role. Here a peasant woman rides a donkey that is pulling her family along the main street of Vilers-au-Flos in May 1916.

Lightly wounded waiting for transport to the rear during the offensive.

A shortage of horses meant that any animal capable of pulling a cart would be used. Here German soldiers are moving around the rear areas using a donkey cart.

than did those of the Allies' and each year it was more difficult to replace the losses.

The position of the German Army at the end of 1916 was ably summed up by the commander of *27 Infantry Division*: 'The formations which were deployed during the Battle of the Somme were very worn down physically and their nerves were badly affected. The huge gaps torn in the ranks could only be filled out by returning wounded, nineteen-year-olds who were too young, or by combing out from civilian occupations, men who, to a large extent, due to their physical condition or mental attitude, could not be regarded as fully effective troops'.

The weather conditions at the end of the year were appalling. Heavy rain and snowfalls, resulting in severe mud, encumbered movement and made life a misery; mud over a metre deep was common; later the conditions were acknowledged to be worse than a year later on the Ypres front. Conditions on both sides of no man's land were equally bad: rifles, caked with mud, were in many cases unusable;

Posing for the photographer, Leutnant Müller, and enjoying the sun, soldiers in the main street of Warlencourt during July 1916.

The Faithful Watch: this photo clearly shows the bond between animals and owners. After an artillery barrage on Achiet-le-Petit in May 1916 that killed his steed, the rider's dog has settled down with the horse.

June 1916 - using a small-gauge railway to bring up the rations.

men sank into the mud and had to be pulled out; with no shelter from the rain, it was almost impossible to maintain health and fitness; illness was rampant among the German troops but there was little that could be done to alleviate the problem of colds, chills, gastro-intestinal illnesses, lung disease, rheumatism and kidney infections. There was no way to ever get dry; it was so wet that one German soldier wrote home that the leather and clothing on the troops were actually rotting while in use. The British *Official History* also makes comment on the conditions: 'the state of the ground of the Somme battlefield during December was such as was probably never surpassed on the Western Front.' It was a wilderness of mud and waterlogged trenches that were accessible only at night. The mud 'took on an aggressive, wolf-like guise, and like a wolf could pull down and swallow the lonely wanderer in the darkness. When it was at its worst no more was feasible than to hold the line.'

However, the bad weather had one benefit: there was little firing and as a result it was possible for troops of both sides to move around freely at times without being shot at; friend and foe could climb out of their holes in broad daylight to stretch their fatigued bodies. But when the weather changed, the artillery would start the war again.

Then on 29 December at 1400 hours the British came again as the history of *6 Württemberger Regiment* noted: 'an enemy patrol approached the right wing of our sector and threw a number of grenades. Our sentries opened fire and brought one of the British down. When our sentries came up to retrieve him he pointed his pistol and refused to give himself up. We took him prisoner anyway and brought him back to our position, where he later died of his wounds. On the same occasion we found another of the British hanging in our wire. He too declined to surrender, and he fell under our rifle fire. Both were of the Grenadier Guards.'

'Germany was hurt more by the Somme than either the BEF or the French' and according to one writer was the 'muddy grave of the German field army, and of the faith in the infallibility of German leadership' but to Jünger 'after this battle the German soldier wore the steel helmet, and in his features there were chiselled the lines of an energy stretched to the utmost pitch.'

'Physically exhausted and emotionally drained, the poor unfortunate infantry of both sides held on in the clinging mud. Cold, icy winds knifed through sleet and driving rain, chilling them to the bone; almost beyond the will to live.' Fortunately for both sides, the battle became stalled in the much hated mud.

Newly arrived troops, before being sent to the front, were camped in emplacements hidden from enemy observation.

Christmas 1916 in a church taken over for use as a field hospital.

Mess facilities and barracks somewhere behind the lines on the Somme front during November 1916.

A dog registration taking place in Manancourt during March 1916.

Local woman studying the latest directive from the Town Commander during September 1916.

When French men were called to the colours in 1914, they left behind their families, thinking they would soon return. Here French children pose for a German soldier in Ervillers during May 1916.

Miraumont, July 1916 – English POWs wait before being taken to the divisional headquarters for interrogation.

A senior Field Medical Officer inspecting a Field Hospital in September 1916.

Even though the Germans were in northern France as occupiers, they still had a responsibility for the public health of the population: inoculation day at Esnes during November 1916.

A soldier's duties were not always military. Bucquoy, October 1916, cleaning out the officers' mess.

Removing a shot-down British aircraft from the rear area where it had crashed in September 1916.

Just as in the previous two years, Christmas was celebrated wherever it could be, with a tree.

Chapter Four

1917

The loss of ground was of no real strategic importance; the importance of the Somme was a moral ascendancy for the Allied forces, and the great losses on the German side. 'It gave the Western Powers confidence. Their armies had accomplished in common an achievement that gave good promise for the future.' While 'the great losses in men, the heavy expenditure of material, ate all too deeply into the strength of the German Army. The immense material superiority of the enemy did not fail to have its psychological effect on the German combatants.' It put a German victory into doubt.

Material losses could eventually be replaced, but high quality soldiers could not. 'The old steadfast highly-trained body of the German Army, particularly in the infantry, had for the most part…disappeared. A great part of the best, most experienced and most reliable officers and men were no longer in their places.' Their replacements, young poorly trained soldiers, were not of the same quality and in

An early casualty in the fighting on the Somme in 1917 was Johann Hartinger, a tenant farmer's son from Weiher, who was killed by enemy artillery on 10 January 1917 while serving in *I Bavarian Reserve Infantry Regiment.*

A railway station well behind the front lines showing the railway transport officers and their female employees.

most cases would never be the equal of the men they replaced.

The preceding months had involved the final stages of the battle of the Somme and the French victories at Verdun, and, as a result, OHL (Oberste Heeresleitung – German Supreme Command) issued instructions on the role of the Siegfried Stellung (Hindenburg Line): 'just as in times of peace, we build fortresses, so we are now building rearward defences. Just as we have kept clear of our fortresses, so shall we keep at a distance from these rearward defences.' A few days later, as a result of the high casualty rate caused by the pattern of defence on the Somme, OHL stipulated that in future defence was to be in depth but elastic. 'Out went deep dugouts and continuous trench lines, to be replaced by concrete bunkers, surrounded by obstacle belts and sited for mutual support. Gone was the rigid holding of the forward trenches packed with infantrymen. In came flexibility, defence in depth, a huge increase in infantry fire power, streamlined command and control and numerous tactical innovations.'

At the end of 1916 the Hindenburg line was to be regarded as a 'factor of safety' and there was no intention of voluntarily retiring to it; however, by the middle of

With the world branding them as barbarians, the German Army was keen to foster an image of concern for the local population. Here two soldiers are being nice to the local children, in an obviously staged pose – neither child looks especially happy about the situation.

To help improve troop morale, Corps HQ had a printing section that produced books as souvenirs for sale to the men. As not all troops could get to their corps headquarters, the book store and lending library came to them when they were out on rest.

January, General von Kuhl summed up the situation at the principal General Staff officers' conference: 'We can no longer reckon on the old troops; there is no doubt but that in the past summer and autumn our troops have been fearfully harried and wasted'.

British Fifth Army winter operations made the situation even worse and, by the end of January, it was acknowledged that the positions presently held by the German Army 'were bad, the troops worn out' and that they were probably not in a condition to stand such defensive battles as 'The Hell of the Somme' again (the 94 German divisions that had fought on the Somme were classed by the British *Official History of the Great War* as being in a "dire state"). After the war the German *Official History* acknowledged the losses of killed and wounded during 1916 as 1,400,000, of whom 800,000 were between July and October. One writer summed up the intensity and sacrifice of the battle after the war: 'whenever you see a fighter who was there at the Somme, bow low to the ground, because you simply do not know what he did for you.' Even with this level of loss and commitment, Ludendorff was not prepared to retire, although 'withdrawal was eminently sensible for a belligerent on the strategic defensive.'

As the war lengthened, telephonic communication became ever more important. This postcard shows a communications bunker where the personnel sleep at their workplace in order to provide a twenty-four hour service.

As Allied air strength grew, aircraft were able to roam behind the German lines picking targets of chance, like these rail trucks, rather than just attacking specific objectives.

With the battlefield churned up by shellfire, the rain turned the ground into slush, making travel difficult and sometimes almost impossible. 'With each step men sank, literally, up to their knees in the mud, of which there were several types. The most bearable was thin mud, because it was less of an obstacle than the thick, clinging sort', which pulled boots off with each step; carrying parties, with their extra weight, were especially prone to this. To make movement easier, men resorted to cutting the bottom half of their greatcoats off because the weight of mud there made movement very difficult.

With the same weather conditions continuing from November and December, life was very difficult on both sides of the wire. St. Pierre Vaast Wood, so hotly fought over in November, stands as an example of the conditions. It was no longer a wood; there were no branches left or stumps, just craters and slushy mud. On the northern side it had become a swamp, dotted with pools of filthy water. Dugouts had been smashed by French artillery or filled with mud, and body parts were scattered over the landscape. With the trenches unusable and an absence of dugouts, troops slept in the open in driving rain or freezing conditions: 'in order to sleep there was no alternative but to sit on a baulk of timber with the upper body covered by a groundsheet. With men standing up to their knees in water,

With Falkenhausen in disgrace, Hindenburg took over command on the Western Front.

A reserve position on the Somme, showing some of the damage done by enemy shelling.

The American entry into the war meant vast numbers of men would be available to help the British and French. It was to be some considerable time before they could make any difference to the war, but their potential number alone was a threat to the German war aims. A French postcard showing the arrival of the first American troops in June 1917 with the message that 2,500,000 of them would arrive by the end of 1918.

German transport moving towards new positions, showing conditions well behind the lines.

living in appalling conditions and not being relieved more regularly, the health of the troops' was deteriorating. One doctor informed his superiors that unless his unit was rotated out of the trenches, the value of the men as fighting troops would rapidly be diminished, and many were likely to be permanently invalided out of the army on health grounds.

The year started, as it was to continue for both sides, with combative action. On 1 January, a British position – Hope Post near Beaumont Hamel - was captured. However, the occupancy was short and on 5 January it was lost along with a neighbouring post and fifty-six prisoners. Further losses occurred on the night of 10 January near Beaumont Hamel when three British bombing parties, independently, carrying 'duckboards to cross the worst of the mud, captured the trenches, some of which were waist-deep in water, taking 142 prisoners.' The next day, Munich Trench fell to a British attack, but the assault by 11 British Division was checked and the positions near Muck Trench held. However, close by, after enduring a two-day heavy artillery barrage, the defending troops in the Beaumont Hamel spur provided little determined resistance, and the British captured around 200 prisoners.

In November, Crown Prince Rupprecht had congratulated everyone on the heroic courage displayed by *First* and *Second Armies* in checking the enemy at every

Some of the belts of wire guarding the new positions of the Siegfried Stellung.

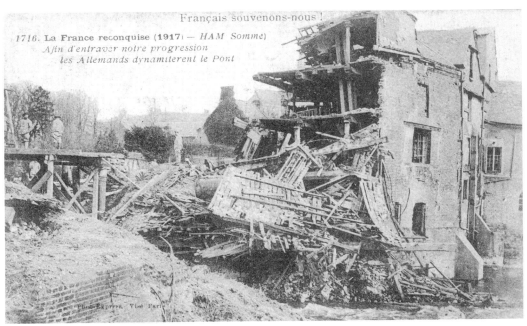

Français souvenons-nous !

1716. La France reconquise (1917) — HAM Somme)
Afin d'entraver notre progression
les Allemands dynamiterent le Pont

A French postcard showing the destruction troops found when they reoccupied Ham: a bridge blown to slow down the French advance.

turn and limiting their gains, for all the effort they put in, to 'a narrow strip of utterly ruined terrain. Everyone who was there can be proud to have been a warrior of the Somme. The greatest battle of the war, perhaps the greatest of all time, has been won.' He was confident that they would stand firm in the face of all future attacks.

Two months later, on 28 January, after a period when frost had made the soldier's life easier in many ways and the second half of the month had been relatively quiet, he demanded a voluntary retirement to the Siegfried Stellung as a result of the British pressure on the Ancre only to be vetoed by OHL.

Further minor British attacks in early February captured a number of useful observation points that stopped the Germans from observing future preparations. On 4 February Operation Alberich was authorised by the Kaiser: retirement to Siegfried Stellung; a retirement on a front 65 miles long with average depth of 19 miles; the whole area to be given the scorched earth treatment. Its objective was to release thirteen divisions (to form a reserve) and shorten the front by around twenty-five miles.

With the certainty of further British attacks, the army was to pull back to the Siegfried Stellung. This defensive line, with a depth of between six and eight thousand yards, ran east from Laffaux to Cerny-en-Laonnais on the Chemin des

A much feared member of the German Army, a machine gunner, proudly displaying his distinctive badge. When the Germans pulled back to their new positions they left behind snipers and machine gunners to slow down the British and French advance. Men such as this caused many casualties.

Zum frommen Gebets = Andenken
an den tapferen Helden Jüngling
Franz Wolsperger,
Soldat beim 10. bay. Res.=Inf.=Regt.
8. Komp.
langjähriger Dienstknecht beim Zenzbauer
in Truchtlaching
welcher am 16. April 1917 im 38.
Lebensjahre an der Somme den
Heldentod fürs Vaterland gestorben ist.

Süßes Herz Mariä sei meine Rettung!
Barmherziger Jesus, gib ihm die ewige Ruhe!
(300 Tage Ablaß.)

Druck von L. Buchner, Altenmarkt.

The British Army kept up the pressure after the German withdrawal. One casualty of the British shelling was Franz Wolsperger of *10 Bavarian Reserve Infantry Regiment* who was killed on 16 April 1917.

A German postcard showing the conditions at the start of 1917 – mud, water-filled shell holes, barbed wire and more mud of which, according to German troops, there three distinct types.

After settling into their new positions, troops could be relieved more often because of the shorter distance to be defended. One popular activity in the summer months was swimming, here in a specially dug pool.

Even in their new positions the German Army was on French soil, so patrols of the rear areas were still needed - a six man patrol during the summer of 1917 somewhere behind the Siegfried Stellung.

In the area being vacated there were a considerable number of civilians who needed to be evacuated to a safer zone. They were generally given a few hours' warning in which to pack what they could carry before they were escorted out of their village. Many would have miles to travel before reaching their new accommodation area, but only a few would be given transport of any description.

A spotter's balloon being positioned to allow an observer to see into the Allied positions and allow accurate reporting of artillery shelling. With no defence, they were an easy target for Allied aircraft unless protected from below by anti aircraft fire. Losses were heavy but their height and a parachute meant that many observers returned to observe again.

When the Germans arrived in 1914 the only civilians they found were females, very young boys and old men. All the men of military age had been called up or left for other towns to work, leaving their dependants behind. This old lady was left behind to look after the farm when her menfolk left.

A toilet review: troops mending, making, cleaning and talking.

Dames ridge where it joined the front-line defences. Three belts of barbed wire protected the trenches, each ten to fifteen yards deep, with a five-yard gap between each. The quality of the barbed wire fences was later to arouse the envious admiration of British soldiers.

The effort put into the construction of the new line was prodigious. A little over ninety miles long and intended to accommodate twenty divisions, the project was scheduled to be completed in just five months. Initially the fortifications were constructed by Russian POWs and later by troops, Belgian civilian conscripts and skilled German craftsmen - eventually around 65,000 men were employed on this task on a daily basis. Not only did it require large numbers of labourers, who needed to be fed, housed and kept in good health but also a new light railway system to get material to the sites had to be constructed. This in turn needed to be transported to the new railways from Germany, placing considerable strain on the German railway system. Over 1,200 trains were used for this purpose between the middle of October 1916, and the middle of March 1917.

'A large number of temporary workshops, goods depots, power stations and hospitals were erected behind the new positions. Despite shortages, only the best materials were used for this building programme. Considerable effort had been put into these fortifications, using mass production techniques: 'all the woodwork

A lorry-mounted mobile anti-aircraft gun preparing to fire. Such guns, provided there were sufficient fuel and spare parts, could be moved quickly around the front, staying invisible to Allied attack because of their mobility.

was uniform in design, the dug-out doors, for example, being turned out to a pattern from the sawmills…by the thousands. Comparatively shallow dug-outs of ferro-concrete…to a fixed pattern and…also mined dug-outs.' Strategically significant, the new line was a triumph of industrial skill and efficient organisation under military control. The work made good progress from the start and there was no reason to doubt it would be ready by the projected completion date.

The new positions were based around the doctrine of flexible defence in depth, and provided a belt of defensive zones rather than a continuous line of defended strong points. 'Each stretch of line had a forward "outpost zone," some 600 yards deep with observation and machine gun posts, plus some concrete dugouts for local counterattack troops.' Behind this was the main battle zone that included the first and second main trench lines, and a network of concrete machine gun emplacements that provided interlocking arcs of fire over no man's land. There were also field artillery positions and vast belts of barbed wire. Counterattack troops, medical personnel and HQ staff were found behind the main battle zone

To entertain troops out on rest, most divisions and corps had their own theatrical troupes. These were the 'Field Greys' a travelling army theatre that moved along the front giving concerts.

Gas was a constant problem in the trenches, particularly after the introduction of the gas shell, so it was essential that troops were fully trained in using their gas masks quickly.

There was always a problem with logistics particularly for an army fighting on more than two fronts. Although under-funded and rapidly wearing out, the German railway system still managed to move materiel relatively rapidly.

Outstanding valour was no protection for a soldier in the field. Franz Marchl, who had been awarded the Iron Cross 2nd Class, the Prinz Luitpold medal and Bavarian Service medal, died of wounds on 15 January 1917. At the time he was a Sergeant in *11 Company* of *4 Bavarian Infantry Regiment* serving on the Somme.

Zur frommen Erinnerung im Gebete
an den tugendſamen Jüngling

Franz Marchl,

Rentamtsdienersſohn von Simbach,
Sergent i. 4. bay. Inf.-Reg., 11. Komp.

Inhaber des Eiſernen Kreuzes 2. Kl., der Prinz-
regent-Luitpoldmedaille, des bay. Militärverdienſt-
kreuzes mit Krone und Schwertern.

Geboren am 1. April 1893.

Er ſtarb den Heldentod fürs Vaterland am 15. Ja-
nuar 1917 infolge einer ſchweren Verletzung
in den Kämpfen an der Somme.

A snapshot taken by a soldier showing the destruction caused by a British shell to his section of the trenches.

in concrete bunkers and dugouts. In places the new positions could be up to 9,000 yards deep.

The real risk involved was that an alerted enemy, pursuing promptly and energetically, could inflict heavy losses on the withdrawing forces. It would be necessary to conceal their intentions from the Allies and withdraw suddenly and to a rigid timetable. Although the British learned of two separate construction sites, there was nothing to connect them and even German deserters and escaped Russian POWs could provide little real information about its design, strength and course. Aerial reconnaissance revealed little due to the poor flying conditions and the strength of the German air force, whose superior planes kept RFC craft inside the original three defensive lines at the front.

By the middle of February, there was insufficient intelligence to suggest the possibility of a German withdrawal over a wide front. A British attack at the end of the month misled British intelligence and confirmed this existing incorrect belief. The success of the British attack on Miraumont, although limited, and continuing British pressure induced Prince Rupprecht to order a local withdrawal to position R1, the first reserve line. An improvised measure outside of the Alberich withdrawal, it confirmed, wrongly, the British intelligence that the Germans were withdrawing to their reserve lines, stage by stage.

There were further reports of withdrawals and, on 25 February, 12 East Yorkshire Regiment sent out a patrol to investigate a report that Serre had been evacuated. Meeting heavy opposition, it withdrew, but a patrol sent out the next day by 11 East Yorkshire managed to get to the German fourth line, only pulling back to the third line because it was not fit to occupy.

It was not until 25 February that the British had a good picture of the new positions in their sector and an idea that there would be a general withdrawal to the new position in one quick operation. But this knowledge was 'too late to make adequate preparations for an effective interference.' In places, British troops moved into evacuated positions before the withdrawal, noting the desolation that stretched to the skyline. The air was still, there was an eerie silence, and the stagnant water in the shell holes gave off a nauseating stench.

The retirement to the new positions was code-named Alberich (a malicious dwarf from the Niebelung Saga) and the Army Group was directed to draw up detailed plans for its execution. Plans were also made to turn the zone between the new positions and the front line into a desert. Only one commander was prepared to condemn these excesses; Crown Prince Rupprecht also threatened to resign at one stage, but was asked to think of national unity and eventually bowed to the pressure.

With gas shells making the accurate delivery of gas possible, every opportunity was taken to provide soldiers with gas drill.

An aerial photo of the battlefield during the winter months mud and shell holes.

With winter over and secure in their new positions, troops found time for essential maintenance and cleaning work.

To make life even more unpleasant for the enemy both sides mixed gas shells and high explosive shells. This photo, taken from German positions, shows a gas and high explosive artillery barrage in action.

The Kaiser was a regular visitor to the front. Here he is inspecting troops somewhere in the Siegfried Stellung during the summer of 1917.

'Not only were all military buildings to be dismantled, depots to be withdrawn, railways to be torn up, craters to be blown in the roads; but so as far as possible, every town and village, every building in them, was to be destroyed by fire or explosive; every tree, even fruit trees, was to be cut down, or "ringed" to ensure that it died; civilians were to be removed; and wells filled up or polluted, though not poisoned.' It was decided to send 125,000 civilians who were fit to work further behind the new defensive line and leave between ten and fifteen thousand civilians - almost all were children, their mothers, and the aged - along with thousands of weapons, items of equipment and buildings carefully booby-trapped to kill or maim the advancing Allied soldiers. This scorched earth policy would hinder the German troops when they returned to the area a year later, creating massive logistical problems for maintenance and re-supply.

Operation Alberich relied heavily on efficient staff work. 'The removal to the rear of installations, provisions and materiel of all sorts…required a large and complex organisation; in the parlous state of the German war economy nothing of any potential value to the army was to be destroyed or left behind…During the five weeks of final preparations for the retreat it was able to accomplish its

A heavy mortar in position in the Siegfried Stellung during August 1917.

The standard German machine gun was very heavy and needed at least two men to pull it. Often it was kept on a sledge to aid movement.

task in the evacuation zone with clockwork precision.' It was a gargantuan task requiring nearly a thousand trains running day and night for the five weeks; 'twenty pioneer companies and ten companies of engineers were needed for the dismantling of the railway installations alone after everything else had been removed.' During this programme civilians were to be left in Nesle, Ham, Noyon and a few smaller places in the intact houses for the advancing troops to look after; the remainder were to be taken away to work in the fields and factories. The programme was scheduled to start on 9 February and end on 15 March. Only then could the troops begin their retirement; by 20 March all troops should be in their new positions. As scheduled, everything was completed by 15 March.

As often with the best-laid plans, all did not go as hoped; British attacks met with stiff resistance, but although prisoners clearly indicated that a retirement would take place in the near future, the severity of the fighting indicated that it would be later rather than sooner on the British Fourth Army front. Conditions were so bad that men who were trapped in the mud died of exposure before they could be dug out. The first withdrawal on the British Fourth Army front took place during the morning of 14 March in secrecy, and it was not until fires were seen burning in St Pierre-Vaast Wood that a forward observing artillery officer crossed no man's land. Over the next two days, the troops withdrew from trench to trench, using sniper fire and machine guns to halt any pursuit. However, by 16

March, the first full marching day, the main body of the troops were retiring to the Siegfried Stellung and by 18 March, four armies were withdrawing on a front of 110 miles, followed by six enemy armies. By the end of March, the complete Alberich timetable was in British hands and they were now aware that the original withdrawals were not part of the plan. The defence line was not wholly complete; indeed, this was the reason for the need to hold on to certain outpost villages. However, by 5 April, the retirement was complete, reducing the amount of line to be defended and increasing the number of men available to counter any future enemy attacks; supply was also easier. However, it was purely a defensive move.

While the High Command advocated defence, the Entente was gearing up for the offence. Both sides were developing tactics designed to make each other's lives more unpleasant. The Germans concentrated on fluid defence in depth, and rapid deployment of local reserves while not countering every attack: the British were developing their use of the 'box' and 'creeping' barrage with little or no preparation, and the night assault. The Somme would now become a quiet front as the battle moved on to Arras, and to the British attack which would be followed by the French attack on the Chemin de Dames.

'On 11 November 1917, Ludendorff presided at a conference in Mons to discuss how a decision could be forced in the west. The conclusion that was reached was that neither the Russian or Italian fronts would affect the ability of the army to deliver a major assault, and that the attack should be at the end of February or beginning of March. Most importantly it must be against the British; if the British Army was broken, as the dominant partner, the French Army would capitulate.' The attack would be against British troops - the next decision was to decide where. After much deliberation Ludendorff chose a fifty-mile front between Arras and La Fère because the ground would dry out quicker than in other British- held areas. The battle would return to the Somme in the coming March.

Chapter Five

1918

1917 had been a hard year but Germany and its armed forces had survived. The future was not all bleak; on the Eastern Front fighting had stopped when a cease-fire had been signed. 'The die was cast, with the release of first-class troops from the Eastern Front 1918 would be the final throw of the dice; a gamble that had to be taken – Germany must win the war before the full entry of American forces onto the Western Front and before grim despondency turned into defeatism.'

'Ludendorff was aware that his manpower reserve was limited and that his forces must therefore rely upon tactical skill instead of sheer weight of numbers and that brain must overcome the enemy's strength. He issued decrees that all troops must undergo special offensive training in accordance with the new hand-book *'The attack in trench warfare'*. Newly arriving divisions from the east passed through the new instructional centres, which trained soldiers, both officers and

Amiens was heavily bombarded during 1918 and was, at one point, the main thrust of the KaiserSchlact.

As the German Army got close to Paris, it was able to use long range artillery to shell the city.

men, before being assigned to a sector as did units already on the front.' The latter were combed for their fittest, most experienced or youngest soldiers which were then formed into storm troop units; in high quality units, the reverse happened and the less able soldiers were sent to other units, in many cases on the eastern front to replace the more able soldiers sent west.

Preliminary orders were issued on 4 January, further orders on 8 February, and final orders on 10 March, for the 'Michael' attack to start around 20 March. This was intended to 'break through the enemy front with the objective La Fère (left flank, Ham-Péronne), and then, in combination with Mars South (Arras front), push forward to Péronne-Arras and beyond. The *Seventeenth Army* with its left wing would carry out Michael 1, in the direction of Bapaume; the *Second Army*, Michael 2 towards Péronne; and the *Eighteenth Army,* Michael 3, towards Ham. The Mars attack (*Seventeenth Army,* right wing) would not take place until several days after Michael, when the artillery required for it was free.' Other assaults were planned for other parts of the front, with diversionary attacks by *Duke Albrecht's Army Group* and dummy preparations and demonstrations carried out to disguise their intentions. But the main attack was to be Michael, supplemented by Archangel and Mars on either flank.

To make sure the offensive was a success, divisions selected only the best and youngest soldiers for élite formations such as the Storm Troops. Unsuitable men were exchanged for better soldiers from units on the Eastern Front.

During the build up of troops it was essential that British and French planes should not fly over the front lines. To maintain secrecy until the last moment, there were constant patrols and much use of anti-aircraft fire.

Even with preparations for the offensive going on, the troops still found time to celebrate the Kaiser's birthday on 21 January.

To the attackers' advantage would be the change of troops that had just occurred: the British had extended their lines south and taken over the French frontage as far as Barisis. This meant that the defenders did not know the area, that their defences would be incomplete, French positions being constructed differently to British ones, and, as the frontage had been lengthened without a corresponding increase in troops, the area could only be thinly defended. On the day of the attack it was foggy, further guaranteeing success to the attackers.

The attackers did not have it all their own way during the days preceding the offensive. Although new to the area, the British were quick to take the war to the Germans. The *Eighteenth Army* found them to be fairly lively, especially their artillery and air force, and as a result, believed that the imminence of attack had been discovered. Although it did not affect the assault preparations, harassing fire fell on the German trenches and a large raid was made on their *III Corps* front just north of St. Quentin.

The attack was to rely on speed of movement by storm troops who would bypass strong points and maintain the momentum of the advance by seeking soft spots. Supporting units would mop up. Into this war of movement was built a carefully planned artillery barrage, the work of Lt. Colonel Bruckmüller. 'The bombardment on 21 March lasted only five hours, its aim being to stun and suppress, not to destroy – and above all – not to forfeit surprise. Its principal

A carefully placed heavy long range artillery piece, ready for the offensive.

target was less the defensive positions of the enemy's infantry than his artillery batteries.'

To reduce the effectiveness of the enemy artillery, Bruckmüller fired tear-gas shells on their positions at the same time as phosgene, forcing the gun crews to take off their gas masks to relieve the irritation to their eyes thereby laying them open to the more deadly gas. Bruchmüller's plan contained a further innovation, the distance the bombardment would reach. To enable this, the artillery would be brought as close to the German front line as possible in order that British back areas could be shelled. Then assembly areas could be contained and unit head-quarters destroyed.

Behind the lines men waited, knowing that a major attack was not far off, but not knowing exactly when they would go into the line. In their billets they checked equipment, rested and chatted. One unit found out when they were to attack, courtesy of the British: an aircraft dropped some leaflets with the message 'Viel Glück zur Offensive am 21. Marz.' Later that day officers received their orders, extra equipment was issued including gas mask filters to protect against tear gas, and a special treat: a hot meal with lots of meat. As it grew dark, the men readied themselves to move out, with the lead troops for the attack moving straight into the front line to take cover in the shelter that had been arranged. They would

Hindenburg, although technically in control, allowed Ludendorff to control the offensive.

Generalfeldmarschall v. Hindenburg
vor seinem Hauptquartier.

The Crown Prince inspecting troops and awarding medals for bravery and excellent service during the summer of 1918.

Joseph Keilhofer, an Unteroffizier in a *Bavarian Pioneer Company*, was a distinguished soldier, having been awarded the Iron Cross 2nd Class and the Military Service Cross with crown and swords. He died while serving near Somme-Py, when a shell hit his dugout on 15 July 1918.

spend the day in the shelters, awaiting the final order to deploy to their jumping-off positions. The plan depended upon an elaborate timetable being adhered to by hundreds of different units. The whole process had to be completed before dawn, to hide from British observation.

The artillery fire was not always one-way and not everything went as planned, as Jünger found out when he brought his company forward on the night of 19/20 March. Everyone was in excellent spirits, even though it was raining, but when they reached what they thought were their quarters, it turned out that the guides had lost their way. Questioning other soldiers they found sitting in shell holes, they found that no one really knew where they were.

Crowding his company into a gigantic crater, he and another officer sat on the edge of another and watched the single shells falling about 100 metres in front. One landed close by, sending splinters into his men's shell hole. As he rushed to check the soldier who yelled that he was wounded, another shell landed in the middle of them all. Picking himself up, although he was only half-conscious, he surveyed the scene to find 'the machine-gun ammunition ...set alight by the explosion, was burning with an intense pink glow. It illumed the rising fumes of the shell-burst, in which there writhed a heap of black bodies and the shadowy forms of the survivors, who were rushing from the scene in all directions.' After a while he collected together what was left of his once proud, fighting fit and full strength company, and found shelter to wait for the attack. He was down to sixty-three men from the 150 he had started with. On returning the next morning, he found over twenty charred and mutilated corpses in a ring around the shell-burst. There were no traces of some who were reported missing.

The activity behind the lines was intense but, to Jünger's amazement, there was little opposition to the build up: 'the first light of dawn revealed an utterly incredible sight. Countless troops, all over the shelled area, were still in search of their appointed shelter. Artillerymen were humping ammunition; trench-mortar men were pulling their mortars along; signallers were laying wires. There was a regular fair a thousand metres in front of the enemy, who, incomprehensibly, appeared to observe nothing.'

The British side knew of the possibility of attack, but the level of awareness varied between local commanders. There were many reports of unusual German behaviour, but, with no specific information about attack time or date, no warnings were given out by the British Third or Fifth armies. But that night a raiding party returned with twelve prisoners who, indicating their desire to be taken to

Storm Troopers, easily distinguished by their grenade bags, were the cream of the German Army, being generally young and fit. Their losses were high and they became increasingly difficult to replace as the offensive progressed.

Losses on the first day of the offensive were high, and the day was not as successful as expected, but British losses were even higher, and many positions were taken. As the troops moved forward so did the artillery, resulting in higher than normal losses among artillery personnel. One such casualty was Josef Leineder, a gunner with *6 Bavarian Reserve Field Artillery Regiment*.

British losses were high during the March attacks, particularly as POWs. Here British troops are being left to find their own way to the rear areas over a wooden road laid specially to allow the easy movement of materiel to the attacking troops.

The basilica at Albert had lost its golden virgin when the Germans arrived; British troops believed that, when it fell down, the war would end – as it did about eight months later. Whether the golden virgin was shot down by German artillery or blown off by the British is unclear, but she never reappeared.

Zerschossene Kirche von St. Albert.

the rear, anxiously told their interrogators that the barrage would start at 0440 hours that morning. Little was done with the information and so, when the attack came, it was still to most units a surprise.

Although the preparations were thorough and the bombardment was to be very intense, the infantry knew that they would have to fight their way through the British positions; although the five-hour artillery attack would destroy artillery positions, wire and trenches, it would not immobilise or destroy the British infantry and machine gunners in their deeper dug-outs.

On the evening of 20 March, the last evening of trench warfare, the men moved forward to the front line, often under fire, found themselves dugouts, officers synchronised watches, men shook hands and wished each other luck and then settled down to wait. Just before zero hour, units received the message that both the Kaiser and Hindenburg were at the scene of operations. At 0505 hours the wait was over; the hurricane broke loose – the artillery barrage had started. Now it was a just a matter of hours before the offensive started, but the barrage eventually brought some retaliation.

Effective counter-battery work enabled the German infantry to assemble without coming under much fire themselves, and, indeed, it provided them a clear view of the pre-battle barrage. 'The enemy artillery was silenced, put out of action by one giant blow. We could not stay any longer in the dugouts. We got out on the top and looked with wonder at the wall of fire towering over the English lines and the swaying blood-red clouds that hung above it.' However, the wind was not always kind and some of the gas fumes blew back on to them, causing fits of choking and coughing. As the artillery reached a crescendo, men ran around shouting delightedly as in front of them was a wall of smoke, dust and gas. Then the large trench mortars joined in throwing two hundredweight bombs at the British lines, and the machine guns joined in too. Then in Lieutenant Junger's sector, with just an hour to go, the British retaliated by bringing a heavy battery into action that dropped shell after shell into his company's crowded trench, killing the battalion commander and a number of men.

At 0910 hours, the officer patrols that were to cover the advance left the trenches and moved forward into no man's land. Many units had already moved forward to get as close as possible to the British lines and, when Jünger and his men moved through their wire, casualties were already moving back. They settled down into a series of shell holes and looking around him, Jünger felt confident of success. 'In shell holes in front of the enemy lines…the attacking battalions were

German rations were inferior to those of British troops and, when the advancing troops came across warehouses and trucks full of food, clothing and drink, many soldiers stopped attacking and celebrated. Here a captured refrigerated railway truck is being unloaded for distribution.

Manacourt château grounds had been a British base before the March offensive.

A captured English tented camp near Avre shortly after it was over-run by German troops.

A heavy British artillery piece captured during the offensive with two of the gun crew, whose boots have been taken by the advancing troops.

A British mobile Vickers machine gun that was hit by German shell fire.

Representative of thousands of men, this picture is of an unknown artillery signals officer who was captured on 22 March.

British trucks hit by the German artillery barrage on 21 March.

A captured British gun position near Bapaume.

waiting massed in companies, as far as the eye could see. When I saw this massed might piled up, the break-through seemed to me a certainty… The decisive battle, the final advance, had begun.'

The fire lifted over the first trenches and at 0940 hours storm troopers clambered out of their shell holes and trenches, and crossed no man's land in groups rather than waves, staying as close as possible to the rolling barrage that preceded them.

The principal blow was against the British Fifth Army that held positions on the Somme. It had only occupied them after the German withdrawal to the Siegfried Stellung a year before, and much of it had been held by the French until a few weeks before the assault. It was also thinly held in defensive positions that were incomplete. Carefully planned the assault was aided by smoke and dense fog that made the attackers invisible until the last minute. Some defenders ran from the onslaught while others stayed and fought to the end, slowing down the attackers.

There were other reasons for the success, clearly identified by British officers who had been captured during the first days of the offensive: strongpoint positions were clearly known, as were battalion headquarters, which were captured in preference; officers were leading their men; artillery was very well handled and close behind the infantry; tanks were used for flattening out wire and clearing up strong points; pioneers followed behind the infantry to bridge trenches and shell-

British officers in a POW camp shortly after being captured in early April. In order to keep them occupied they were provided with material to allow them to put on a show for the other officers.

holes for ease of movement. In addition British SOS rockets could not be seen in the fog; the bombardment had damaged all the cables so there was no inter-unit communication possible; and low flying aircraft flew in advance of the infantry firing their machine guns into the trenches and at gunners who had to keep their head down.

The success of the day is clearly shown by the number of British casualties – 38,512 – of whom 21,000 were taken prisoner. But the attackers did not get as far as they expected, even though confusion among the British command increased German gains over the next two days, as British troops fell back. By 24 March the British had been pushed back, on average, fifteen miles, and had lost about 50,000 men as POWs.

The greatest success was enjoyed by *Eighteenth Army* that had opened a serious gap in the British line; in less than a week the most successful units were pushing forty miles into the British lines. Although this was a significant distance, it was not in the area where the breakthrough was really needed – the advance was

A captured British artillery shell dump at Péronne.

The result of a direct hit on a British truck during the March offensive.

British six-inch artillery piece captured near Manancourt in March 1918.

moving in the wrong direction. All that was being won was a very large salient – there was no real prize to be won. Even though the advance threatened Amiens, this was never taken and the railway centre continued to supply the British with men and materiel.

On 23 March, the decision was made to that the three armies should operate divergently north-westwards, westwards and south-south-west respectively; this was a change of plan. Previously the main thrust had been against the British by *Second* and *Seventeenth Armies,* with the *Eighteenth Army* protecting them from French attack. Now the attack was being shifted to the left in three directions with three objectives: separating the French from the British, driving the British into the sea, and defeating the French.

Supply was also a problem. 'Provisioning the attackers before the offensive had been difficult with only four days' supply of ammunition available instead of the five days originally planned; food was also short. One soldier wrote home and complained that there was bread but nothing to go with it and that some soldiers were so hungry that they take 'any bacon or ham you might have that has gone mouldy.' What had not been possible before the start of the offensive was now proving to be even more difficult; there was insufficient horse-drawn or motorised transport to successfully cross forty miles of devastated land, and not enough engineer troops to repair roads, lay new rail tracks and provide sufficient light railway stock. The further the army advanced, the more difficult it was for the commanders to keep in touch with their men due to a shortage of telephone wire – as a result orders could take a day to get where they were needed. On top of these internal logistic problems, there was always the British air force to contend with. Although British aircraft losses were greater than German ones, the sheer number of British planes gave them overall air supremacy, and as a result they were able to bomb and strafe military transport columns as they traversed the forward battle zones and also attack infantry positions and reinforcements.'

All had not gone to plan and there were still considerable difficulties to overcome, but the Kaiser was overjoyed by what he thought was a victory, ordering the flags to be flown and a victory salute to be fired to celebrate his army's triumphs at Cambrai, Monchy, La Fère and St. Quentin on 25 March. 'As a reward for the success of the offensive he awarded Hindenburg the Iron Cross with Golden Rays (the last recipient of the award had been Field Marshal Blücher in 1814) and Ludendorff the Grand Cross of the Iron Cross. Many officers quietly felt that the Kaiser was being overly optimistic.' After the war, Captain Goes described 25 March as the day when 'the sun of Germany's victory was high in the zenith' - but expectation and reality were not the same.

'The offensive continued but huge losses, exhaustion and the lack of a decisive

British heavy mortar taken in March. This postcard was produced by a Leipzig publisher to celebrate the advance.

British POWs in a temporary camp at Gouzeaucourt, while awaiting transportation to Germany.

A six-inch field gun and trailer captured in its gun pit.

British ammunition limber discarded during the retreat.

British shell dump captured intact during the advance.

breakthrough anywhere, linked with an ever increasing length of supply chain and a shortage of all types of supplies were taking their toll on morale, resulting in low spirits and incidents of disobedience and drunkenness when British supply dumps and French towns were overrun. "Binding recorded in his post-war memoirs what he had seen in Albert after 3 Marine Division had looted the town: there were men driving cows before them on a line; others who carried a hen under one arm and a box of note-paper under the other. Men carrying a bottle of wine under their arm and another one open in their hand…men dressed up in comic disguise. Men with top hats on their heads. Men staggering. Men who could hardly walk at all." Accusations about divisions not pursuing the British troops because of drunkenness were later shown to be untrue, it was found to be the determination of the British defences that was the key issue in checking the advance.'

On 27 March the troops pushed in the direction of Amiens, gaining ground but unable to achieve a decisive breakthrough, and they were eventually stopped about seventeen kilometres short by 31 March. Indeed, some senior officers regarded the day as the turning point of the offensive. Crown Prince Rupprecht, finding that the *Second* and *Seventeenth Armies* were not progressing as expected, asked for the three reserve divisions to be sent to the right wing of the latter army. His comment after his request was refused was very telling: 'then we have lost the war.' The attack of the *Seventeenth Army* was then temporarily stopped

German shelling and British explosives meant that many bridges had been destroyed. Here advancing troops cross a river using a temporary wooden structure.

until the Mars attack against Arras, due the next day, had improved the situation. The other two armies were to push on with their attack.

The failure of Operation Mars put the onus temporarily back on the Somme while preparations were made for a more northerly offensive against the British and later against the Belgians. *Second Army* was to increase pressure south of the Somme and would be reinforced by two divisions from *Seventeenth Army* that, along with the *Seventh* and *Eighteenth Armies*, was to stand fast while the left wing of the *Second Army* pushed on towards Amiens.

On 29 March, *Eighteenth Army* stopped its forward movement on the greater part of its front and found itself subject to ever more vigorous counterattacks. In the afternoon, Ludendorff gave instructions for the continuance of the attack on Amiens south of the Somme and beyond the line Chauny-Noyon-Montdidier, with the left wing of *Second Army*, the *Seventeenth Army* and right wing of the *Seventh Army*. The remainder of *Second* and *Seventeenth Armies* would later join in the attack north of the Somme. *Eighteenth Army* issued the order: 'The enemy for the moment has only inferior or beaten troops opposite us. Reinforcements are said to be approaching him…They must not be permitted to engage according to plan. The *Army* will attack tomorrow with all possible force.'

Ludendorff's original aim of the reduction of the British Army had now been

Heavy artillery pieces were kept well behind the lines prior to the attack to stop them being seen by the British. This is a 21cm Howitzer park with the guns, wagons and limbers ready to move forward.

The ruins of Péronne Cathedral after the battle had moved on.

British dead awaiting burial.

reduced in scale to a local tactical operation: the capture of a railway centre – Amiens. Lacking strategic vision, Ludendorff was following the line of least resistance in order to keep the offensive moving and, as he perceived that 'in the direction of Amiens the enemy's resistance seemed weaker', it became the objective. The attacks further south, near Montdidier, were diversions to hold enemy forces; all efforts would now be directed towards Amiens. The extreme left wing of *Second Army* took possession of Demuin and the passage of the Avre River at Moreuil, but, further north, little was achieved. *Fusilier Regiment 86* from Schleswig Holstein, part of the first rate *18 Infantry Division*, took part in the unsuccessful attacks and noted that 'the power of attack was exhausted. Spirits sank to zero. The division suffered a reverse the like of which it had not yet experienced.'

Writing after the war, Hauptmann Goes noted that: 'the fighting during the closing days of March had left no doubt that the great offensive battle was threatening to become a battle of attrition on the largest scale. Everywhere along the long front of nearly 120 miles, the infantry had been compelled to have recourse to the spade, and saw the spectre of hated position warfare rising before it.' They would have to start from scratch if it happened. There were 'no trenches, no dugouts, streaming rain for days, which had turned the devastated area behind the troops into a morass, and caused the roads and tracks, laboriously rendered serviceable, to break up again.' They knew that they were fighting an enemy with greater reserves than they had and regularly received reports of new divisions arriving to attack the salient they had created. 'More and more the artillery swelled in volume; higher and higher rose the losses of the Germans in dead, wounded and sick, and more and more did the spirit of their attack evaporate.'

Preparations went ahead for the Lys attack, but one further attack on Amiens was scheduled, with the arrival of reinforcements and replenishment of ammunition stocks. For three days, operations on the front were suspended while troops prepared themselves for the next battle.

After the respite, the attack was pushed forward again on 4 April and, on the French section, took Morisel and Mailly-Raineval, threatening the railway from Clermont to Amiens. In the north, finding resistance stiffening, the troops withdrew onto the Villers-Bretonneux plateau but, next day, after vigorous counterattacks, took back the lost ground. It had been intended to press on to Amiens on both sides of the Somme, but little was actually done and the day was a failure. In his war diary, Crown Prince Rupprecht noted that the offensive had now come to a complete stop and, without careful preparation, would not be successful. Ludendorff ordered the attacks stopped because 'the enemy's resistance was beyond our powers. We must not get drawn into a battle of attrition.'

With the enemy so close, the French decided to evacuate all civilian inhabitants on 9 April because of the danger caused by artillery shelling. That same day, *Fourth*

A photo taken in 1919 showing the destruction caused during the fighting of 1918.

A captured British long range artillery piece captured intact during the March offensive.

and *Sixth Armies* launched their attack, Operation Georgette, on the Lys front. Things were already beginning to move away from the Somme.

Between 15 and 19 April local French offensives cleared the railway but, after a violent bombardment on 24 April, the attack was resumed, this time against the junction between the British and French at Villers-Bretonneux and Moreuil. Villers-Bretonneux was captured from the British, but French troops were able to hold onto Hailes until after bayonet fighting in the streets of Hangard, when the position was lost. At the same time, a more limited attack was carried out on French positions on the Moreuil bridgehead, with the object of taking the heights north west of Castel. 'It not only brought the desired gains of ground, but numerous prisoners.'

Two days later, an Anglo-French counterattack from Villers-Bretonneux to the valley of the Luce forced the German troops back to their start lines. However, Amiens was still in danger of shelling from long-range railway guns and was in fact regularly shelled until the start of the Allied offensive on 8 August.

'When Operation Michel was suspended the Germans found themselves in defensive positions on the muddy Somme battlefield that they had voluntarily left a year earlier. Although the assault had cost them more casualties than they had inflicted, they had captured 90,000 Allied soldiers and 1,300 artillery pieces and, in terms of distance, *Second Army* had advanced forty-five kilometres and *Eighteen*

The long range gun used to shell Amiens shortly after the offensive began.

Army up to sixty kilometres. However, the success had created its own problems in terms of supply, there was now a very large salient that was vulnerable to counterattack in certain places, the plans now being adopted were tactical rather than strategic and the casualties could not be replaced in either number or quality; a problem that the British did not have with over 100,000 trained soldiers ready for use in France before the end of the month, the French army had lost little of its fighting strength and had now recovered from its problems of May 1917 plus there thousands of Americans arriving on a weekly basis. The French Army intelligence service had also noted the deteriorating quality of the German front line soldier since 21 March.'

And when the battle moved north to Flanders, the problems did not go away. Supplies did not get through, the number of good quality soldiers decreased and the British and French did not give in. By April the Somme was again comparatively quiet as attention was focused around Ypres. On his return to the front after recovering from his wound, Jünger found himself back on the Somme where by June plants were reclaiming the land. The ground was still cluttered with the remnants of the battle: 'shell-shot wagons, abandoned ammunition, the weapons of hand-to-hand fighting, skeletons of half-decayed horses, surrounded by the hum of myriads of flies.' In this strange landscape, burned-out tanks became tourist spots.

The main focus of the war might have moved away, but the British did not stop shelling the Germans in their new homes. Although not heavy, the bombardment caused casualties, and sickness, in the form of influenza, made worse by undernourishment, meant that troops spent longer in the front line awaiting the inevitable attack as the bombardment increased.

After the March offensive, the German thrust had moved to Flanders and, when this failed to deliver the much-needed breakthrough, the French were to receive the next offensive. Having already suffered 400,000 casualties in the previous assaults, the German Army delivered a surprise attack on the Chemin des Dames on 27 May. Only with great difficulty was this stopped, thirty-six miles short of

German soldiers climb the ruins of Bapaume church during the March offensive.

A propaganda comparison of the five month British Flanders offensive and the first seven days of the German March offensive.

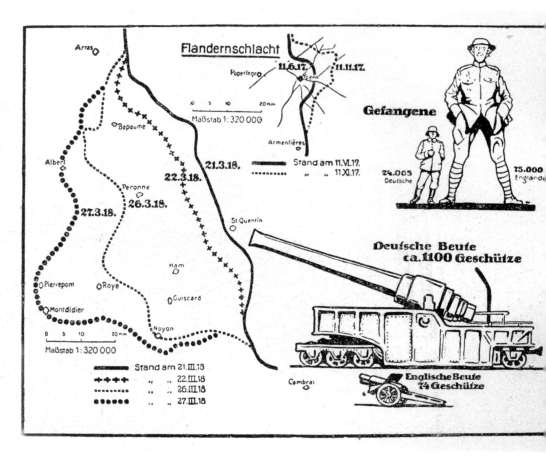

5 Monate englische Flandernoffensive
7 Tage deutsche Offensive und ihre Ergebnisse

Flandernschlacht

11.6.17.   11.11.17.

Arras

Poperinge   Ypern

Maßstab 1:320000

Armentières

Bapaume

Albert

Peronne

22.3.18.   **21.3.18.**

26.3.18.

27.3.18.

St Quentin

Ham

Pierrepom   Roye

Guiscard

Montdidier

Noyon

0 5 10 20 km
Maßstab 1:320000

Stand am 11.VI.17.
11.XI.17.

Gefangene

24.005 Deutsche   75.000 Englände

Deutsche Beute ca. 1100 Geschütze

Cambrai

Englische Beute 74 Geschütze

Stand am 21.III.18
"   " 22.III.18
"   " 26.III.18
"   " 27.III.18

German reserves marching towards Albert.

The remains of a section of the British line between Bapaume and Arras.

British dead in a trench near Albert.

Captured British position hidden under a railway embankment.

A British artillery battery shelled while in a sunken road near Clery.

The remains of a British tank after being shelled near Albert.

A British heavy artillery piece captured near Ham.

A British Field Artillery battery over-run near Albert.

Paris. Ludendorff mounted his next attack just two weeks later, on 9 June, against the French between Noyon and Montdidier; the war had briefly returned to the very southern end of the Somme.

A sudden increase in the number of German deserters on 7 and 8 June confirmed French suspicions that the attack was imminent and a deserter on the night of 8/9 June gave exact details of the offensive timetable, allowing the French time to organise their artillery counter-preparation. This caught some of the divisions forming up and disrupted their formation for the attack. However, the German artillery barrage that followed was a 'Bruchmüller orchestration', starting with gas and then high explosive to stop the French artillery, while trench mortars destroyed the wire and front line positions. By careful shelling of key positions and bridges, the area was isolated. In defiance of orders, French commanders had placed nearly half their infantry within 2,200 yards of the front — the area the artillery had just bombarded. Trenches had been obliterated, men buried, and survivors staggered like drunken men; in consequence the first German assault met little resistance. By evening they were over the Matz on a wide front, having advanced six miles, taken over 8,000 POWs and virtually wiped out three French infantry divisions. The next day the advance continued and, when a French division collapsed, causing another to pull back, it exposed the French right wing to attack. The next day the French launched their own attack, using tanks. By 13 June, after further vigorous French counterattacks, the assault was halted and German attention turned to Operation Friedensturm, an attack on the Marne. Once again the Somme became a backwater of the war.

The second battle of the Marne came as no surprise to the French who had excellent intelligence about its strength, aims and timings. As part of their defensive preparations, they intended to launch their own offensive. Although two French deserters gave the Germans accurate details of the attack, the intelligence was passed around too slowly to make any difference. The attack was a complete surprise and, as a result of this and the strength of the attack, the Germans in the path of the French Tenth Army fell back. This battle, which dragged on until 7 August, was the last offensive action of the German Army in the war. Now the Allies were on the offensive.

Amiens was to be the site of the beginning of the end of the war on the Western Front. The final German offensive had been stopped and the Allies now had the advantage. After a series of smaller attacks along the front, the Allies launched an attack on 8 August that Ludendorff called a 'black day' for the German Army; after this there was no way to defeat the enemy – it was a matter of time and what terms could be gained.

At 4.20am on 8 August, Australian, British and Canadian troops, assisted by a devastating artillery bombardment, 800 aircraft and over 400 tanks, launched

Two captured tanks near Clery; before long, and after a little cannibalising, one or both would be ready to attack the British.

An intact four-inch howitzer captured in Roisel.

Two British railway guns captured near Péronne.

Heavy artillery shells in a dump near Aubigny.

themselves at the *Second Army*; by lunchtime Allied success was virtually complete. The German official account of the war acknowledged that it was the greatest defeat since the start of the war with an estimated loss of up to 700 officers and 27,000 men, of which about seventy percent were POWs. On 10 August, there were signs that the Germans were pulling out of the salient created by Operation Michael.

According to official reports, by 27 August, the Allies had captured nearly 50,000 prisoners and 500 guns. Even with the lessened number of tanks the British had advanced 12 miles (19 km) into German positions by 13 August.

The first phase of the battle ended on 11 August, and by then Germans had retreated to the lines they had held before the first battle of the Somme; lines Haig felt were too strong to attack without a proper artillery bombardment as tanks could not be used because the old Somme battlefield was a wasteland of shell craters. In the fifty days from 8 August to 26 September, the British pushed forward an average of twenty-five miles on a forty-mile front, compared with an advance of eight miles on a twelve-mile front in four and a half months in 1916.

The high losses meant that there was no longer the manpower to rebuild the broken divisions. While not strategically decisive because the Allies were unable to exploit its success, the battle was quite decisive in the moral sphere; 'it deprived not only Ludendorff but German soldiers at company level of all faith in final victory.'

On the same day as the Amiens battle started, further south in the Somme region, the French attacked at Montdidier. A series of preliminary actions had forced the Germans to abandon their bridgehead west of the Avre, securing an excellent starting point for the main French attack and allowing forward movement of the artillery. On a twenty-one mile wide front, the French positioned ten divisions in the front line, three army corps in the second line and five divisions in reserve, while 600 planes would provide support. Facing them were eight divisions in the front line and six in reserve. All these divisions were reliable – any unreliable division had been replaced.

The French attack, slow to start, developed rapidly, although in places there was considerable confusion: bridges were too narrow for the tanks, tanks ran out of petrol and second – line units advanced too early. Moreuil was taken, but, by nightfall, even though the French had taken 3,500 POWs and moved up over five miles, the main objective had not been reached. Despite reinforcement, the Germans were unable to hold the Allied advance on 9 August and were pushed back to their 1914 positions on the Matz. The next day Montdidier was re-occupied during the seven-mile French advance. Subject to numerous counterattacks from 11 August onwards, the French advance was severely hampered.

The French planned to resume the offensive on 20 August with an attack towards the Somme River in the north and the Lassigny-Noyon line in the south

German troops searching through the remains of a British ration dump, effectively slowing down the advance.

Pleased to be out of the war – British POWs await orders after being captured near Bapaume. Most of these men appear to be 'Bantam' soldiers. Men under the normal height for enlistment.

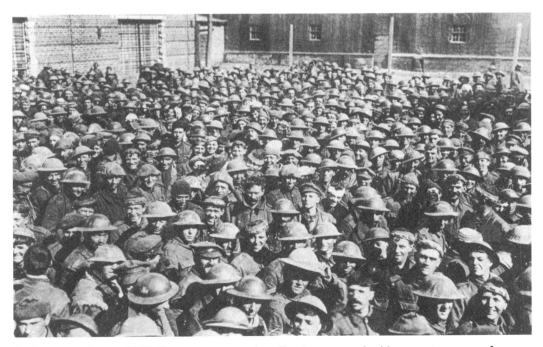

As large numbers of POWs were expected, collection camps had been set up away from the active areas. This one, to the south of Arras, held 4000 soldiers who were waiting for transport to take them to Germany.

Ready for immediate tenancy, the British camp at Avre was taken almost complete.

in order to push the Germans back to their 21 March positions. By 27 August, Roye and Chauny had been taken. The offensive had been a success and, coupled with the Tenth Army's attacks, helped push the Germans further back towards the Siegfried Stellung. Yet the hoped-for extent of the advance was never realised, and the German front line was never actually broken. The victory was strategical rather than tactical.

Instead of continuing at Amiens, Haig launched a second attack further north, using the Third Army and part of the First Army; its purpose was to force the Germans back to the line of the Somme. The attack began on 21 August with the Battle of Albert that lasted until 31 August; this was then followed by the Battle of Bapaume from 31 August to 3 September.

On the front north of Albert, three British Corps of three divisions each, faced eight German divisions strongly entrenched between the Somme and the Scarpe. Using heavy artillery, tanks and ten squadrons of aircraft, the three corps attacked just after first light, partially hidden by the morning mist. Two of the corps were immediately successful, but the third corps was held through the skilful use of the swampy areas along the Ancre. The next day, a fourth corps attacked and obliterated the German salient between the Somme and the Ancre and recaptured the ruins of Albert, setting the stage for the general advance on 23 August in which the Australians cleared the Germans from the valleys about Chuignes. They forced them to evacuate the bend of the Somme and leave behind the fifteen-inch railway gun that had been used to shell Amiens. North of Albert, despite attacking numerically stronger positions, the British troops took all their objectives. 'Although the German machine gunners continued to resist with their normal skill and courage, there were now signs of a continuing decline in German morale.' Despite a change in the weather, the advance continued, even though the Germans had pushed a further eleven divisions into the fighting. By the evening of 25 August, British troops were approaching Péronne and Bapaume.

An attack near Arras that pushed the German troops back four miles, coupled with the fighting on the Somme, made Ludendorff realise that he must abandon Bapaume and the whole devastated area north and west of the Somme. On the night of 26/27 August, orders went out from his headquarters for a gradual withdrawal to a line behind the southern bend of the Somme from Péronne to Ham and south to Noyon. 'This still left him between 15 and 20 miles' elbow room in front of the main Hindenburg defences, except near Arras where the line already joined the main position.'

Over the next three days, the German troops gradually withdrew to the new line and, as during the previous withdrawal in 1917, they left any shelters booby-trapped and often fouled. The usual indication that withdrawal was imminent was a great increase in artillery fire as gunners used up their ammunition. Actual with-

Many bridges were damaged during the advance and heavy artillery created large shell holes. Here, pioneer troops are repairing the damage caused by a mine somewhere between Ham and St. Quentin.

drawals were covered by increased fire from high-velocity guns firing at long range. Single-gun detachments in woods and copses augmented the interlocking fire of well-sited machine guns, leap-frogging backwards only when threatened by infantry envelopment.

As a result of the withdrawals on 29 August, New Zealand troops captured Bapaume and by the night of 30 August, Australians made the next breakthrough, fighting their way across the Somme. At 0500 hours, on 31 August, a much-depleted Australian division attacked Mont St. Quentin, a mile north of Péronne; German resistance was extremely stiff and only a foothold on the hill was taken. After four days of ferocious fighting, and reinforced a day after the start of the attack by a further division, the Australians captured Péronne. Another Australian division had pushed the Germans out of the Bouchavesnes spur in equally bitter fighting.

While the Australians were fighting on the Somme, the Canadian Corps, fighting with the First Army, broke through the Drocourt-Quéant switch, south east of Arras on 2 September. At the same time the French continued their attacks further south. This series of events resulted in the issuing of orders for a general retirement in gradual stages to behind the Sensée and the Canal du Nord and, further south, to the Siegfried Stellung; the whole salient won in March was to be abandoned.

It was not until several hours after dawn on 3 September that it was noted that the Germans had started to withdraw. Following on behind the withdrawing Germans, the British infantry encountered only light resistance and by evening were approaching the Canal du Nord. Knowing that taking the new positions could be difficult, Haig ordered his commanders not to undertake large-scale operations, just maintain contact with the Germans and allow as many men as possible to be rested and trained for the attacks on the Siegfried positions.

The army falling back on the Siegfried Stellung was 'badly shaken, rapidly deteriorating owing to casualties and lack of sleep' and, since 21 August, divisions had disappeared from the order of battle and replacements could only be found by breaking up others. However, at the sharp end the army was still being well handled, and in many cases was still prepared to fight to the end as the men withdrew to their new defences. 'At night the sky was red with the flames of burning villages: the days were punctuated by the dull thud of ammunition dumps being blown up behind the German lines.'

The war had moved on from the old Somme battlefields to the Siegfried line and the last battles of the war. It would not return until May 1940 when the story would be entirely different.

Chronology of the Somme Front 1914 – 1918

1914

17 September General Bridoux, commanding officer of French I Cavalry Corps, killed in a raid on supply lines east of Péronne – General de Mitry takes over on 30 September.

25 September Battle of Albert begins; Catelnau driven out of Lassigny-Noyon area.

26 September First battle of Picardy ends: Castelnau halted at Ribecourt-Roye-Chaulnes-Bray-sur-Somme line to await formation of new Tenth Army on his left. *XIV Corps* takes Bapaume from French.

29 October French repulsed near Roye, Lassigny and Chaulny, and checked before Thiepval.

1 October Fighting around Roye; French line holds.

8 October Fighting renewed at Roye.

5 November French repel attack at Le Quesnoy-en-Santerre.

29 November French advance at the River Chaulnes.

19 December Attack near Lihons repulsed by French.

1915

2 January Positions lost near Vermelles to French attack.

17 January Limited French advance north of the river at La Boiselle.

3 February Incendiary filled boats floated across the river Ancre fail to dislodge French troops.

11 April Heavy fighting near Albert.

7 June Salient into French positions at Touvent Farm between Hébuterne and Serre, lost on a two-mile front when attacked by part of French XI Corps; French troops hold positions and counterattack fails.

13 July Newly formed British Third Army relieves French Second Army of fifteen-mile sector from River Somme to Hébuterne.

29 December At the first conference between Joffre and Haig, a summer offensive on the Somme is first suggested using sixty-five divisions on sixty mile front from Arras to west of Peronne-Lassigny.

1916

29 January *Second Army* successful against French positions northeast of Dompierre.

6 February Positions at Vache Wood and Signal (Frise) lost to French attacks between 6 and 13 February.

23 March British trench raid on positions at Gommecourt.

4 April General Micheler takes command of French Tenth Army previously on Arras Front.

11 April Attack on British positions at La Boiselle repulsed.

25 May Proposal by *Second Army* Chief of Staff for a pre-emptive attack to counter Allied build-up on the Somme Front ignored.

11 June Allied offensive advanced from July to 29 June.

24 June British artillery opens up the preliminary barrage - 2029 guns firing 1,732,873 shells (with about one in three failing to detonate) damaging or destroying 109 guns. Between 24 and 30 June, the BEF makes seventy trench raids and forty gas attacks.

28 June Due to rain, British attack postponed until 1 July.

1 July Anglo-French offensive begins at 0730 hours with 224,221 shells being fired in sixty-five minutes and ten mine explosions. Nineteen divisions attack on a twenty-five mile front north and south of the Somme. Mametz and Montauban lost to British infantry with French troops pushing to Hardecourt and Curlu, taking 3000 POWs and about eighty guns. British attacks on other parts of the front partially or fully repulsed.

2 July Fricourt lost to British attack, and *12 Reserve Division* night attack to recapture Montauban fails. South of the Somme, Herbecourt, lost to French attack.

3 July Ovillers-La Boiselle and Bernafay Wood lost to British attacks. As a result of the losses, General Below replaces his Chief of Staff.

4 July Two villages south of the Somme lost to the French, who now hold six miles of second line trenches and have taken 4000 POWs.

5 July Horseshoe Trench stormed by British troops. Estrées, south of the Somme, recaptured from French. Infantry columns strafed by British aircraft.

7 July British attack on Mametz Wood repulsed, but Contalmaison lost later that night and Leipzig redoubt lost.

8 July Shelling and counterattack push British troops back from Trônes Wood. French Foreign Legion attack on Chancellor's Trench fails, but is lost on 1 August.

9 July Biaches and Hill 97 with La Maisonette lost to French, who repulse the counterattack.

10 July Remains of Contalmaison village lost to British attack. After severe fighting in Mametz Wood, troops pushed back and Wood is lost on 12 July. Twenty-six guns and 7500 POWs lost to British so far in Somme offensive.

11 July Contalmaison counterattacks repulsed by British.

12 July Further counterattacks against Contalmaison repulsed.

13 July Battle of Albert ends.

14 July After a five-minute bombardment on a three and one half mile front followed by a surprise dawn attack, positions in Bazentin le Petit and Longueval are captured by British troops who take 2000 POWs; Trônes Wood lost to British attack.

15 July South African Brigade attack and take Delville Wood and hold out for five nights and six days of counterattacks by three divisions and shelling by 180 guns. RFC bombs thirteen targets for no loss.

17 July Waterlot Farm, east of Longueval and Ovillers, lost to British attacks.

18 July Strong counterattacks against British positions at Longueval and South African troops at Delville Wood repelled.

19 July *Second Army*, north of Somme becomes *First Army* under General F Below. Outflanking movement at Delville Wood compresses South African position but fails to take it. Likewise attacks on British positions at Longueval, Trônes Wood and Waterlot Farm are also unsuccessful.

21 July Falkenhayn laments that no more troops from quiet sectors can be used to feed the Somme Battle until relieved by 'fought out' divisions and that seven such divisions are required to replace those already transferred to the Somme.

22 July Counterattacks against French positions south of the Amiens-Peronne high road repulsed. Heavy fighting along the front from Pozières to Guillemont.

23 July Pozières village lost to an Australian attack and most of Delville Wood recaptured.

24 July Counterattacks against British positions at High Wood and Guillemont unsuccessful. After twenty-four days of fighting against the British, the forward positions were generally three and one-quarter miles back on a six-mile front with the loss of over 11,000 POWs.

27 July British continue to attack positions in Delville Wood, at Longueval and near Pozières.

28 July Delville Wood and Longueval lost to British attacks.

29 July Two counterattacks fail to push British troops back at Delville Wood. Australian attacks on the Windmill position are repulsed.

1 August Attack north of Bazentin-le-Petit against British positions fails. Heavy, inconclusive fighting on the Thiepval salient.

2 August Further attacks against British positions in Delville Wood fail.

3 August Troops fail to hold British attack west of Pozières.

4 August Second line trenches on a 2000 yard front north of Pozières and 1750 POWs lost to British and Australian attacks.

5 August British make slight advance east of Pozières.

6 August Fighting at Mouquet Farm.

7 August British positions north and northeast of Pozières attacked, while British attack the outskirts of Guillemont.

8 August British troops attack Waterlot Farm and Guillemont where troops are pushed back to the southern end of the village but resist any further attacks.

9 August Casualty return for *18 Reserve Division* shows the intensity of the fighting – over fifty percent casualties (8288 of all ranks) since 24 July.

12 August Counterattack on British positions in High Wood unsuccessful but troops unable to hold British attacks on a mile front northwest of Pozières.

13 August During the day-long artillery battles north and south of the river, Munster Alley is lost to British troops.

16 August Defending troops fail to hold French attacks along the river and lose trenches on a twelve-mile front and 1300 POWs. West and southwest of Guillemont, British troops make limited advances.

17 August Northwest of Bazentin, trench lost to British forces and counterattack northwest of Pozières fails to recapture British positions.

18 August British attack on High Wood held but troops fall back after British assaults towards Ginchy and Guillemont.

19 August British troops advance to Thiepval Ridge.

21 August British make slight gain in the fighting for Thiepval and advance on a more than one-mile front northwest of Pozières.

22 August Counterattacks against British positions at Guillemont repulsed.

24 August Bavarian troops lose Maurepas to French Frère Battalion (1 Regiment of 1 Division) and British advance towards Delville Wood and Thiepval.

25 August Delville Wood taken by British troops and attacks against British positions south of Thiepval are repulsed.

26 August Heavily fortified Mouquet Farm lost to Australian attack.

28 August *Army Group Crown Prince Rupprecht* created. *Second Army* artillery return shows that since 26 June 1068 (out of 1208) field guns and 379 (out of 820) heavy guns have been captured, destroyed or become unserviceable.

29 August Kaiser dismisses Falkenhayn (Chief of Staff) replacing him with Field Marshall Hindenburg and General Ludendorff as his assistant. Since 1 July British have taken 15469 POWs and captured eighty-six guns and 160 machine guns.

31 August British troops defending Delville Wood repulse four attacks. Fifty-one aircraft lost on Somme front since 1 July.

1 September East side of Delville Wood recaptured from British, but four counterattacks against High Wood fail.

3 September French Sixth Army, north of the Somme, captures most of Cléry and the defences along the road north to Le Forest and Le Forest village. Guillemont and part of Mouquet Farm lost to heavy British attack. Defending troops repulse British attacks on Schwaben redoubt and High Wood.

4 September British attacks on Falfemont Farm repulsed. Heavy fighting on five-mile sector against French troops who gain Soyecourt.

5 September British capture Falfemont Farm and link with French across Combles ravine whilst French take Ferme de L'Hôpital and Ommiecourt.

6 September Ten counterattacks against French positions southwest of Barleux and south of Belloy smashed by French artillery and British take Leuze Wood and advance to Ginchy.

8 September Hindenburg and Ludendorff visit the Western Front for the first time.

9 September Ginchy lost to British attacks. Counterattacks against French positions around Berny recover some lost ground.

10 September Counterattack on British positions at Ginchy fails and troops east of Guillemont fail to halt British advance.

11 September Munitions dump at Grandcourt destroyed by British artillery.

12 September Bois d'Anderu and Bouchavesnes lost at start of French offensive.

13 September Heavy counterattacks fail to dislodge French troops at Bouchavesnes and French advance southeast of Combles.

14 September The Wonderworks and trenches southeast of Thiepval stormed by British troops and French take Le Priez Farm.

15 September 146 extra heavy guns sent to *First* and *Second Army* and 144 worn-out guns replaced. After forty minute barrage fourteen British divisions, including two Canadian and the New Zealand Division, with tank support advance behind a creeping barrage on a six mile front capturing Flers, Martinpuich, Courcelette and High Wood, and by 1000 hours are in the third line trenches. British Guards division is held up by the defenders of the 'Quadrilateral'. Later in the afternoon, the French attack north of Priez Farm makes only slow progress but further south captures three villages.

16 September Hindenburg orders construction of the Siegfried Stellung. Five relief divisions now available to counter any British attacks. Dunibe Trench lost, New Zealanders advance north and west of Flers, while counterattack against British in Courcelette fails.

18 September 'Quadrilateral' lost to depth of 1000 yards and French gain ground around Combles in two local evening attacks.

19 September Counterattacks east of Cléry during the night fail to dislodge French troops.

20 September Attacks against British positions at Bouchavesnes almost succeed.

21 September Starfish Trench, Cough Drop Alley and a section of Flers line lost to British attacks.

22 September Flers-Courcelette battle ends and British advance east of Courcelette.

23 September Ground lost to British attack east of Martinpuich.

24 September Counterattack on British positions west of Lesboeufs fails.

25 September Rancourt, Les Priez and Frégicourt lost to French Sixth Army while British troops, supported by two tanks, capture Les Bouefs and Morval and almost surround Combles. Troop trains at Libercourt and Lille stations attacked by RFC.

26 September Using tanks, British troops capture Thiepval. British and French troops take Combles and Grid Trench. Using tanks and aircraft together, British troops capture 500 yards of trenches at Guedecourt. A number of infantry surrender to a RFC contact patrol aircraft and troop positions strafed by RFC fighters.

27 September After hand-to-hand fighting, the ruins of Thiepval are lost to the British who also advance north of Flers.

28 September Defending troops fail to hold French attacks at Morval, and British attacks against Schwaben Redoubt and positions northeast of Courcelette.

29 September Strongly fortified Destremont Farm lost to British attack.

30 September The six divisions from Le Transloy to the Ancre replaced by nine divisions from other parts of the Western Front. Over seven million rounds fired and 127 counterattacks made against Allied positions during September.

1 October 128 divisions now opposing Entente forces. British advance between Eaucourt and Le Sars and begin attacks on the Ancre Heights.

2 October Counterattack pushes British troops out of Sars.

3 October Eaucourt lost to British attack.

5 October Troops fail to hold British advance northwest of Eaucourt and French attacks east of Morval.

7 October Strong resistance fails to halt Franco-British attack on the Albert-Bapaume road and positions on the Butte de Warlencourt heavily attacked.

8 October Counterattack takes Regina Trench and the 'Quadrilateral'.

9 October British advance east of Le Sars towards Butte de Warlencourt and Stuff Redoubt lost.

10 October French attacks northwest of Chaulnes take 1400 POWs; counterattacks on the Bois de Chaulnes result in the loss of a further 1702 POWs.

12 October Since 1 July, 40125 POWs taken by the French. Further British attacks on a four-mile front between Eaucourt-Bapaume gain between 500 and 1000 yards.

14 October Schwaben Redoubt taken by British troops and French make gains on a 1½ mile front south of the River Somme.

15 October Attacking troops of *First Army* supported by 333 aircraft, and British pushed back at Schwaben Redoubt and Thiepval.

18 October Battle of the Transloy Ridges ends; British advance north of Guedecourt and French take Sailly. French attacks at La Maisonette pushed back.

20 October Heavy attacks on the British defences in Schwaben and Stuff Redoubts repulsed.

21 October British advance between Schwaben Redoubt and Le Sars takes 5000 yards of trench and 1018 POWs; Stuff Trench also captured by British.

22 October French capture ridge west of Sailly.

23 October British capture 1000 yards of trenches towards Transloy.

28 October British troops make slight progress against defences northeast of Lesboeufs.

29 October Dewdrop and Hazy trenches captured by Allied troops.

1 November French repulse counterattack at Sailly-Saillisel and then advance northeast of Lesboeufs. Since 1 July, 72901 soldiers lost as POWs, along with 303 guns, 215 mortars and 981 machine guns.

2 November British capture trench east of Guedecourt.

5 November See-saw action with British near Butte de Warlencourt. French capture most of Sallisel and attack St. Pierre Vaast Wood. Counterattack succeeds in retaking Bayonet Trench, taken earlier in the day by ANZAC troops.

7 November British gain ground east of Butte de Warlencourt and repulse counterattack against Beaumont Hamel. French capture Ablaincourt and Pressoir south of the Somme and repulse counterattacks on the two villages.

8 November Counterattack against Sallisel makes slight gains, but after heavy fighting over the next three days French capture the whole village. Australian positions north of Geudecourt strafed.

10 November British capture eastern section of Regina Trench (north of Thiepval) and French capture some trenches northeast of Lesboeufs.

11 November Ancre Heights battle ends; British capture Farmers Road near Regina trench.

13 November Battle of the Ancre begins at 0545 hours with British attacking with ten divisions; Beaumont stormed by the attackers taking 1200 POWs

— St Pierre Divion and Beaucourt captured as British troops push defending troops back a mile. About 360 men of *3 Battalion 62 Regiment* buried alive by explosion of 30000lb ammonal mine at Hawthorn Crater.

14 November British capture Beaucourt taking 400 POWs, and RFC artillery observation planes direct gunfire that kills well over thirteen hundred soldiers.

16 November British advance east of Beaucourt but lose some ground east of Butte de Warlencourt.

18 November British gain a 1000-yard deep bulge on three-mile front. Since the start of November, losses stand at 45000, against British losses for November at 46238.

26 November Instructions issued on Siegfried Stellung.

1 December *OHL* issues first manual on defensive warfare, emphasising defence-in-depth and organic development from the Somme Battles where defence had quickly become deeper.

11 December Violent Allied artillery barrage.

31 December At the end of the year 127 divisions, each equipped with forty-eight mortars, face106 French, 56 British, 6 Belgian and 1 Russian divisions.

1917

1 January Hope Post near Beaumont Hamel captured from British.

5 January British capture two posts near Beaumont Hamel.

9 January Trenches east of Beaumont Hamel lost to British.

10 January British attack takes trenches on a ¾ mile front northeast of Beaumont Hamel.

17 January Four counterattacks fail to eject the British troops who had captured 600 yards of trench north of Beaumont-sur-Ancre.

27 January 350 strong garrison lost to British attack near Le Transloy.

28 January Crown Prince Rupprecht demands a voluntary retirement to the Siegfried Stellung as a result of the British pressure on the Ancre, but this is vetoed by OHL.

31 January Counter-attacks on British positions on the Ancre repulsed. BEF claims over 1200 POWs taken during January.

1 February Fifteen battalions and two companies of *Stosstruppen* (shock troops) serving on the Western Front. Each infantry company is to be provided with three light machine guns (Bergmann LMG) as soon as possible. Trench raid on British positions at Grandcourt repulsed. British trench raid near Guedecourt takes 56 POWs. Senior commanders and staffs attend Solesmes tactical school to learn new defence methods.

3 February British advance 500 yards east of Beaucourt, taking over 100 prisoners.

4 February Operation Alberich authorised by the Kaiser: retirement to Siegfried Stellung; 65 miles long with average depth of 19 miles; whole area to be given the scorched earth treatment. Objective: release thirteen divisions and shorten front by twenty-five miles.

6 February Grandcourt evacuated after British occupy 1000 yards of trenches.

8 February Hill 153 (Sailly-Saillsel ridge) lost to British troops along with 78 POWs.

9 February Operation Alberich commences: demolitions and programmed removal of materiel and civilian population.

10 February Counterattack fails to regain 1250-yard trench system south of Serre Hill from the British; 215 POWs lost during initial attack.

11 February 600 yards of trenches near Beaucourt-Puisieux road lost to British.

17 February British attacks at Miraumont result in 773 POWs and up to 1000 yards' loss of front during the two attacks.

18 February Attacks on British positions above Baillescourt Farm repulsed.

19 February South of Le Transloy, attack with flamethrowers captures British post and 30 POWs.

22 February Retirement to Siegfried Stellung accelerated due to British pressure, with a preliminary withdrawal of three miles on a fifteen-mile frontage.

24 February Troops pull back evacuating Serre, Miraumont, Petit Miraumont, Pys and Warlencourt.

25 February British and Australian attacks on Les Thilloys (southwest of Bapaume) start, and continue until 2 March.

27 February Villages of Ligny and Le Barque on the Somme lost to British attacks.

28 February Over the month, eleven villages and 2133 POWs lost to British attacks.

1 March Army command structure reorganised with battalion strength being reduced to 750 from around 1080 thus giving 1422 battalions – 1289 during September 1916.

2 March Counterattacks near Bapaume fail to hold Les Thilloys, and further territory is lost northwest of Puisieux and north of Warlencourt.

3 March British advance east of Gommecourt.

4 March Bouchavesnes lost with 217 POWs; six counter-attacks fail to regain the village.

10 March Irles and Grévillers Trench lost along with 292 POWs.

13 March British advance 1½ miles from Bapaume with further losses to British attacks east and northeast of Gommecourt.

14 March Main withdrawal to the Siegfried Stellung begins, with British following cautiously.

15 March French troops advance in the south and British advance on a 1½ mile front between St. Pierre Vaast Wood and Sallisel.

16 March First marching day of Operation Alberich - synchronised withdrawal to Siegfried Stellung begun by thirty-five divisions; St. Pierre Vaast wood occupied by British troops.

17 March Bapaume occupied by Australian troops – all public and commercial buildings blown up and secret mine underneath; BEF occupies a total of thirteen villages and French occupy Roye.

18 March Allies enter Nesle together while French enter Noyon, finding the streets mined and booby-trapped, and the BEF enters Chaulnes and Péronne, finding the wells to the southwest poisoned with arsenic.

19 March Withdrawal completed by twenty-nine divisions.

24 March Roisel, east of Péronne, occupied by British troops.

25 March Mine under the Town Hall in Bapaume explodes, killing nearly thirty.

1 April Savy and Savy Wood, four miles west of St. Quentin, lost to British attacks.

3 April French occupy seven villages near St. Quentin.

5 April Majority of troops now positioned in the Siegfried Stellung with Allied pursuit impeded by bad weather, collapse of roads, demolitions, booby traps and rearguard troops.

18 April Villers Guislain captured by British.

20 April Gonnelieu captured by British.

21 April Limited local losses due to British attacks.

10 May Troops fall back on south bank of the Scarpe after British attacks.

26 May First US troops disembark in France.

29 May Skirmishing with British troops near St. Quentin.

5 June British attack north of the River Scarpe.

18 July Trench raids southwest of St. Quentin repulsed by British.

19 July Further attacks against British St. Quentin sector.

1 September British positions at Havrincourt near Cambrai are captured and occupied before British counterattacks push troops back.

2 September Attacks against British advanced outposts near Havrincourt fail.

9 September 600 yards of trenches at Villeret, and 400 yards northwest of St. Quentin, lost to British troops.

1 October Army strength on the Western Front now stands at 147 divisions with 12,432 guns (against 16000 Allied guns).

18 November Trench raids on British positions northwest of St. Quentin.

27 December General Hutier from the Eastern Front takes over the new *Eighteenth Army* at St. Quentin.

28 December Both sides raid positions north of St. Quentin.

30 December Parts of Welch Ridge lost, and counterattacks the next day repulsed by British troops.

31 December Over 180,000 US troops now in Europe.

1918

10 January French troops in the St. Quentin area are relieved by the British.

21 January Spring offensive decision taken.

22 January British trenches near St. Quentin raided.

26 January British replace French from St. Quentin to Barisis, south of the Oise.

28 February Western Front strength now 180 divisions.

1 March Advance parties start to move up for spring offensive.

3 March Some British positions raided.

5 March New cipher introduced prior to offensive.

9 March British and French positions between Ypres and St. Quentin bombarded with 500,000 Mustard and Phosgene gas shells.

10 March Operation Michael ordered by Hindenburg.

16 March Most artillery in position for offensive, and infantry begin night approach marches.

17 March Two deserters tell British XVIII Corps to expect six-hour barrage but have no date.

18 March Hindenburg and Ludendorff move forward from HQ at Spa to Avesnes.

19 March Troops issued with special gasmask filters, twenty anti-tank bullets and grenades ready for start of offensive. Near St. Quentin, troops bombarded by the British with eighty-five tons of Phosgene, causing over 1000 casualties.

20 March 190 divisions now available on the Western Front.

21 March Operation Michael – British Fifth Army attacked on forty-two mile front and British Third Army on a forty-three mile front. *Storm troops* attack in dense mist and advance up to 4½ miles against fierce resistance; attack assisted by tanks. Advancing troops take 21,000 POWs, over 500 guns, forty-six villages and more territory than was lost on the Somme in the July - December 1916 offensive. Ludendorff aims to cut off British from French. British losses 38512 against attacking troop losses of 39929.

22 March Attack continues with fresh troops moving forward, pushing British troops further back, taking another 16,000 POWs and 200 guns; Epéhy and Roisel captured and Crozat Canal crossed.

23 March Troops take Ham and Péronne. Paris shelled by three 8.26inch guns at range up to seventy-four miles, killing 256 and injuring 620.

24 March Enemy pushed back and troops cross the Somme between Ham and Péronne, and further south capture Chauny rail junction. British cavalry attack at Villeselve captures three machine guns.

25 March British counterattack beaten off at Bapaume, and Nesle and Noyon captured. British Fifth Army pushed back about four miles on a twenty-three mile front; enemy front now fractured.

26 March *3 Marine* and *54 Reserve Divisions* enter Albert and take Roye from the French. British light tanks halt advance in Colincamps-Hébuterne area, routing two attacking battalions.

27 March British hold up advance to the Somme and Amiens at Rosières.

29 March Offensive starts to slacken along Ancre north of the Somme.

30 March Moreuil Wood lost to British counterattack, but further south French troops fall back on a twenty-five mile front, losing six villages.

31 March Since the start of the offensive 75,000 POWs taken and about 1,000 guns. Moreuil Wood retaken from British troops.

1 April Heavy but inconclusive fighting at Albert, Grivesnes and Hébuterne.

3 April Local fighting in Hébuterne and Scarpe sectors.

4 April New 5-letter field cipher cracked by French.

5 April *50 Prussian Reserve Division* advances nearly a mile on the Ancre Front, but British counterattack near Hébuterne takes 200 POWs. Somme offensive ends.

6 April Further severe inconclusive fighting around Albert and Hébuterne.

23 April Heavy attacks against British positions at Albert and between the Somme and the Avre.

24 April Villers-Bretonneux taken, along with nearly 400 POWs, by two divisions and thirteen tanks. A7V tank 'Elfreide', knocked out after disabling two British machine gun tanks in the first tank battle. Night counterattack by British troops retakes Villers-Bretonneux.

1 May There are now 204 divisions on the western Front. US units reach Amiens sector.

5 May British advance at Morlancourt between the Ancre and the Somme.

9 May Some territory is yielded to French troops attacking at Grivesnes, northwest of Montdidier.

10 May Front line trench northwest of Albert lost to British attack.

11 May British positions on the Ancre shelled.

14 May Attack on a mile front southwest of Morlancourt successful, but ground lost to enemy counterattack.

16 May British raid trenches near Beaumont Hamel.

18 May During the night of 18/19, Australians capture Ville-sur-Ancre and take 360 POWs.

25 May Artillery bombardment of Villers-Bretonneux.

28 May In the first US offensive operation, Cantigny is captured and all counter-attacks repulsed.

1 June Between 1000 and 2000 cases of flu reported per division.

11 June Australian troops capture 300 POWs during a peaceful penetration.

22 June Enemy tanks and infantry raid trenches at Bucquoy in first night tank attack.

4 July British and American units advance on a 3½ mile front to a depth of 1½ miles capturing Hamel, two guns, 171 machine guns, two mortars and 1472 POWs. Northeast of Villers-Bretonneux troops pushed back 2000 yards.

7 July Two Austrian divisions arrive on the Western Front. Some ground lost north and south of the River Somme to Australian troops.

12 July Castel-Auchin Farm captured by the French. Fifth offensive postponed.

29 July Australian advance on a two-mile front at Morlancourt, taking thirty-six machine guns and 138 POWs.

31 July 313410 US troops land in France.

3 August Troops withdraw behind the Ancre.

4 August Withdrawal in the Somme Sector on a ten-mile front between Montdidier and Moreuil on the east bank of the River Avre.

5 August Paris bombarded by long-range gun for the final time.

6 August Divisional counterattack at Morlancourt regains much ground and takes 250 British POWs.

8 August The black day of the Army in this war – British attack at Amiens, routing five divisions and taking nearly 900 guns and over 29,000 POWs.

9 August British advance on the Somme continues but at a slower pace, capturing Morlancourt.

10 August Montdidier garrison surrounded and captured by French Army during seven-mile advance. Seven new divisions arrive to stem Allied advance. Drunken Bavarians shout at *38 Division*: 'What do you war-prolongers want?'

11 August Counterattacks stabilise the Amiens front. Ludendorff offers his resignation to the Kaiser who refuses to accept it.

12 August Australians take Proyart.

14 August Decision taken to evacuate the Ancre Sector. Ludendorff recommends immediate peace negotiations.

15 August British troops cross the Ancre. Counterattack around Damery repulsed by Canadian troops. French troops take the Lassigny Massif and the town.

16 August Troops pushed back in Roye Sector by Anglo-French attack.

21 August British attack on a ten mile front at Albert, using tanks, aircraft and smoke, pushes defenders back between two and three miles for the loss of 2000 POWs - counterattack repulsed.

22 August Albert lost and counterattacks repulsed.

23 August British attack on thirty-three mile front, taking 7000 POWs, and in some areas push the defenders back up to two miles; further British attacks at night.

24 August Thiepval Ridge and Mory Copse are lost to a British attack.

25 August Further enemy advance takes Mametz Wood and two villages north of Bapaume.

26 August Army Group Commanders ask for permission to withdraw seventy miles to the Antwerp-Meuse position; Ludendorff allows a ten-mile withdrawal on a fifty-five mile front during the night.

27 August Greenland Hill and Delville and Trônes Woods captured by British troops. French recapture Chauny and Roye.

28 August General retirement from the Scarpe to above the Aisne. French reoccupy Chaulnes.

29 August New Zealanders recapture Bapaume.

30 August Australian Corps crosses the Somme south and west of Péronne.

31 August Péronne captured. Heavy fighting on Mont St. Quentin with *2 Guard Division* losing 700 POWs during the Australian attack. Overall losses since the start of the enemy offensive amount to 228,000 with only 130,000 replacements available; ten divisions disbanded to stiffen remainder.

1 September British attacks eliminate Amiens salient. Mont St. Quentin captured.

2 September Ludendorff issues order for a second phased retirement to the main defences behind and along the Canal du Nord.

3 September At Epenancourt, south of Péronne, French troops cross the River Somme.

4 September Ruyaulcourt, seven miles east of Bapaume, captured by New Zealand troops.

5 September French attack on the Somme pushes defenders back across the Crozat Canal and captures Ham and five other villages.

7 September Roisel rail junction, on the Cambrai to St. Quentin line, captured by British.

9 September The high ground at Havrincourt Wood, overlooking the Siegfried Stellung, is captured by British troops.

13 September Anglo-French forces close in St. Quentin.

15 September Construction of Hermann line begun.

18 September Enemy assault, on a sixteen-mile front, northwest of St. Quentin, results in the loss of Epéhy and 9000 POWs.

24 September High Command informs the government that armistice talks are inevitable. Over 30,000 men lost as POWs in the last week to the British alone. Further attacks push defending troops back to within two miles of St. Quentin.

25 September Counterattacks near Epéhy, against British positions, repulsed.

29 September Thirty-nine British and two US divisions attack against 41 defending divisions on a twelve-mile front. Kaiser approves Hindenburg and Ludendorff's request for an armistice. Anglo-French units attack the Seigfreid Stellung after a bombardment of nearly one million rounds. British cross the St. Quentin Canal using boats, ladders and lifebelts, advancing 3½ miles and taking 4,200 POWs.

30 September Only fifty-nine of the 197 divisions now classed as fit. Ten divisions disbanded to provide troops for other divisions. Medium batteries reduced from four to three guns due to a shortage of horses. Bulgaria signs an armistice to end hostilities.

1 October Ludendorff sends a cable to Berlin government to transmit a peace offer without further delay.

2 October French enter a ruined St. Quentin.

3 October British troops with tanks attack the Beaurevoir Line on an eight-mile front, capturing Le Catelet.

4 October Troops fall back on the Kriemhilde positions.

5 October British capture Beaurevoir and troops withdraw from the Scheldt Canal. The order of the day from the Kaiser mentions a peace offer, but urges the army to continue to offer stern resistance.

8 October Enemy attack on a twenty-mile front between St. Quentin and Cambrai, taking the Fresnoy-Rouvroy line, Forenville, Niergnies and Villers-Outreaux along with 10,000 POWs; three local counterattacks using 4ATV tanks and captured British ones fail to recapture lost villages near Cambrai. *Army Groups Boehn* and *Rupprecht* ordered back to Hermann position – *Boehn Group* to be split up and used by other armies.

9 October Canadians enter Cambrai and British drive towards the River Selle.

24 October Ludendorff asks men for continued resistance.

26 October Ludendorff resigns and is succeeded by Gröner. The Kaiser refuses Hindenburg's resignation.

30 October *18 Landwehr Division* refuses to go back in to the front line. Turkey signs an armistice, with hostilities to cease from 31 October.

3 November Austro-Hungarians sign an armistice with hostilities to end on 4 November.

8 November Armistice delegates meet with Foch.

9 November The Kaiser abdicates.

11 November Armistice signed and hostilities cease at 1100 hours.

13 November Troops begin general retirement to Germany.

14 November Munitions dump south of Namur blown up by retiring troops.

18 November As the last troops leave French territory, a munitions dump east of Namur is blown up.

22 November Last troops leave Luxembourg.

26 November Final troops in Belgium cross into Germany.

Zur frommen Erinnerung im Gebete
an den tugendsamen Jüngling

Eugen Hartinger
Gymnasialabsolvent

Einj. Gefr. u. Off.-Aspirant,
Masch.-Gew.-Führer im K. B. Res.
Inf.-Regt. Nr. 19
geboren am 29. August 1898 in
Göbelsbach, für das Vaterland
gefallen am 16. Juli 1918.

Süßester Jesus, sei mir nicht Richter, sondern
Erlöser! (50 Tg. Ablaß)

Mein Jesus, Barmherzigkeit! (100 Tg. Ablaß)

Süßes Herz Jesu, sei meine Liebe! (300 Tg. Ablaß)

Süßes Herz Mariä, sei meine Rettung! (300 Tg. Ablaß)

Eine größere Liebe hat niemand als diese, daß
er sein Leben hingibt für seine Freunde.

Herr, Du hast ihn uns gegeben. Du hast ihn
uns genommen, Dein heiliger Wille geschehe.

Ich habe den guten Kampf gekämpft, den Lauf vollendet, den Glauben bewahrt. II. Tim. IV., 7, 8.

Although the war on the Somme had quietened down since March, there were still casualties, one of whom was nineteen-year-old Eugen Hartinger. He was serving as a Gefreiter in charge of a machine gun section with *19 Bavarian Reserve Infantry Regiment* when he was killed on 16 July 1918.

The only Germans on the Somme after the war were the dead – and POWs many of whom were kept there to help clear up the debris of war.

Bibliography

Becke, Major A.F. Military Operations France & Belgium, 1918 volume 1. Macmillan & Co, 1935

Bilton, D. The German Army at Arras, 1914-1918. Pen & Sword. 2008

Bilton, D. The German Army on the Western Front 1917-1918, Pen & Sword. 2007

Chickering, R. Imperial Germany and the Great War, 1914-1918. Cambridge University Press, 2005

Duffy, C. Through German eyes: the British and the Somme 1916. Weidenfeld & Nicholson., 2006

Edmonds, Brigadier General Sir James, CB, CMG. Military operations France & Belgium, 1915. Macmillan & Co, 1928

Edmonds, Brigadier General Sir James, CB, CMG. Military operations France & Belgium, 1916. Macmillan & Co, 1932

Edmonds, Brigadier General Sir James, CB, CMG. Military operations France & Belgium1918, volume 1. Macmillan & Co, 1935

Edmonds, Brigadier General Sir James, CB, CMG. Military operations France & Belgium1918, volume 2. Macmillan & Co, 1937

Edmonds, Brigadier General Sir James, CB, CMG. Military operations France & Belgium1918, volume 5. HMSO, 1947

Falls, Captain C. Military operations France & Belgium 1917. The German retreat to the Hindenburg line and the battle of Arras. Macmillan, 1940

Foley, R. German strategy and the path to Verdun. University Press Cambridge. 2005

Goes, Captain G. Die grosse Schlacht in Frankreich 21 Marz – 5 April 1918. Kolk, 1933

Görlitz, W(ed). The Kaiser and his Court (the First World War diaries of Admiral Georg von Müller). Macdonald. 1961

Gray, R & Argyle, C. Chronicle of the First World War. Volume 1, 1914 – 1916. Facts on File, 1991

Gray, R & Argyle, C. Chronicle of the First World War. Volume 2, 1917 – 1921. Facts on File, 1991

Hull, I. Absolute Destruction. Cornell University Press, 2005

Jünger, Ernst. The Storm of Steel. Chatto & Windus, 1929

Kitchen, M. The German Offensives of 1918. Tempus, 2005

Ludendorff, General. My War Memories 1914-1918 volume 2. Hutchinson (No Date)

Middlebrook, M. The Kaiser's Battle. Allen Lane, 1978

Miles, Captain W. Military operations France & Belgium 1917. The battle of Cambrai. HMSO, 1949

Passingham, I. All the Kaiser's men. Sutton Publishing, 2003

Rickard, J. www.historyofwar.org. Battle of Amiens, 8 August-3 September 1918. 2007

Sheldon, J. The German Army on the Somme 1914 – 1916. Pen & Sword, 2005

Strachan, H. The First World War. Volume 1: To Arms. Oxford, 2001

Strachan, H. The First World War. Simon & Schuster, 2003

1940 and the German Army arrives at the Somme again.

When the war with France was over the old defences became tourist spots for photos to to send home.

Although the fighting was not as heavy as in the Great War there were still losses. The photos show a soldier paying his respects to a fallen comrade, a wayside grave, and the beginning of a military cemetery.

Sterbeurkunde

(Standesamt Wedel (Holstein) – – – – – Nr. 67/1916)

Unteroffizier, Arbeiter Hinrich Gustav Wilhelm Stüven – – – – – – – – e vangelisch – –

wohnhaft in Wedel, Hinter der Kirche 13 – – – –,

ist am 5. August 1916 – – um – – – – – Uhr – – – – – – Minuten

in der Schlacht an der Somme verschüttet und verstorben.

D er Verstorbene war geboren am – – – – – – – – – –

in Wedel – – – – – – – – – – – – – – – – – – –

(Standesamt – – – – – – – – – – – Nr. – – – –)

Vater: Arbeiter Johann Hinrich Stüven in Wedel – – – – – – – – – – – – – – – – –

Mutter: Catharina Dorothea geborene Wichmann – – – in Wedel – – – – – – – – – –

D er Verstorbene war – nicht – verheiratet mit Margaretha Catharina Elisabeth geborene Kock in Wedel – – – – – – – – – – – – – – – – – – –

Wedel (Holstein), den 9. Juni – – – – 1943

Der Standesbeamte

In Vertretung: Klatt

C 251, C 252. Sterbeurkunde (mit Elternangabe bezw. ohne Elternangabe).
Verlag für Standesamtswesen G. m. b. H., Berlin SW 61, Gitschiner Straße 109. C. 2775 (a.2)

C 251 | C 252

A 1943 death certificate (Sterbeurkunde) issued at Wedel, in Holstein, proving the death of Hinrich Gustav Wilhelm Stüven. Unteroffizier Stüven, born at 13 Hinter der Kirche in Wedel, serial number 67/1916 was buried by shellfire and died on 5 August 1916 during the fighting on the Somme. A labourer like his father Johann, Hinrich was married but had no children when he died.